MONOGRAPH SERIES

SHARPSHOOTER:
Hiram Berdan,
his famous
Sharpshooters
and their
Sharps Rifles

by

WILEY SWORD

ANDREW MOWBRAY INCORPORATED/*publishers*
P.O. Box 460, Lincoln, Rhode Island 02855   U.S.A.

LIBRARY OF CONGRESS
CATALOG CARD NO.: 88-062056
   Wiley Sword
     Sharpshooter
   Lincoln, RI: ANDREW MOWBRAY INCORPORATED — *PUBLISHERS*
     128 pp.

ISBN: 0-917218-37-X

Printed in the United States of America

TABLE OF CONTENTS

Colonel Hiram Berdan, ca. 1863 (National Archives)

PREFACE

"It was the most critical moment in my life," reflected the grizzled sixty-four year old former combat veteran. Confronted by what seemed to be a line of enemy skirmishers behind trees 150 yards ahead, and detecting the movement of other enemy troops in their rear, he had pondered what to do. "I reasoned to myself that I was ordered to find the enemy. I have done so....I will [thus] retire and give the alarm." But, no, "it occurred to me that the enemy would [advance]...almost as soon as I could get back to our lines...."

Although overcome by "that awful feeling that this would be sure death to me," an "all inspiring feeling...forced me to decide to fight,...for we must have time at any cost....I then gave the order — 'Follow me, advance firing!'."

Twenty six years later, as he helped dedicate a monument at the same spot, an unbowed Hiram Berdan reflected, "no act of mine gives me so much pleasure."[1]

Was he a hero of Gettysburg, the courageous and perceptive leader of the famed reconnaissance to Pitzer's Woods that alerted the Army of the Potomac to the danger of a pending flank attack on July 2d? Or, as another has said, was he an inveterate liar and a flagrant fool, always careful to stay out of harm's way, and so lacking in military expertise as to have unnecessarily exposed his men at Gettysburg during a failed reconnaissance? "I want to bear testimony...to the unlimited cowardice" of this man, wrote a highly incensed corporal of an earlier action. He "loses what little coherency there is about him when he is placing men in position, and takes excellent care to be far in the rear before there is a possibility of being shot."[2]

Hero or scoundrel, brilliant or incompetent, Hiram Berdan in retrospect seems to have been perhaps a little of each. Certainly, he was a prominent if often controversial figure, a man whose legacy eventually became even larger than the flawed but capable individual he appeared to others to be.

Hiram Berdan's fortune was his fame, which seemed to become an ardent ambition. While egocentric and highly ambitious, the man's talent as a mechanical engineer, as a gifted inventor, as a top rifle shot, and as a man of connections were impressive and genuine.

These attributes, however, were frequently matched by his excessive vanity, petty actions, conniving manner, and want of personal courage on the battlefield. He was, in fact, a man both to be much admired and somewhat pitied. His genuine friends were few, but ardent in their praise. Berdan's enemies were perhaps more numerous, many being his subordinates who were bitter about their treatment, but not about his many abilities. Berdan's men, to their credit, recognized both the good and bad qualities, for they reaped the fruits of each.

Berdan's regiment, and later his demi-brigade of sharpshooters, were probably the most famous unit to have served in the Federal Army. The historian William F. Fox wrote in 1888 the much quoted remark that Berdan's sharpshooters "undoubtedly killed more men than any other regiment in the Army." This statement has stood well the test of time and modern research of Civil War records. Moreover, the sharpshooter "corps" recruited under Berdan's direction became truly the unique organization of the war. Conceived under an innovative concept, to fight not as an infantry unit, but as skirmishers and snipers well in advance of the line of battle, there were few units more effective in their combat role, or more personally feared by the enemy.[3]

This "corps of sharpshooters" was actually two separate regiments, the 1st and 2d U.S. Sharpshooters, but the second unit was an outgrowth of the first, being a surplus of companies organized to serve with the original regiment. Popularly, both in and out of the Army, both units became widely known as Berdan's Sharpshooters. Justifiably, their story is many stories — the story of the man who commanded them, the story of the men who fought and earned such high honors, and certainly not least, the story of their famous Sharps rifles that firmly established the efficacy of breechloading small arms in combat.

PART I:
HIRAM BERDAN — THE MAN

Hiram Berdan was a man of many accomplishments which followed from a variety of endeavors; farmer, mechanical engineer, soldier, inventor, and large scale business entrepreneur. Wealth was his forte even at a young age. Yet mostly it was his keen and discerning mind that was the essence of the man. Highly intelligent and innately curious, his intuitive grasp of mechanical engineering, his easy, quick calculations, and a capacity for practical reasoning early marked this Michigan youth for important success.

Although he was born at Phelps, New York, September 6, 1824, Berdan's family had moved to what is now Plymouth, Michigan (then little more than a wilderness farm community) when Hiram was about six years old. Because the Berdans were farmers, their young son had grown up with nature and a love for the outdoors. An old Detroit resident who had known him at the time, reflected years later about Berdan's "strong and healthy" boyhood. "He excelled in all boyish sports," and "passed every leisure hour in the woods with his rifle," the man remembered.

Indeed, although Berdan had left the farm in the late 1840's to pursue an engineering career, his rural Michigan background was ever reflected in his lifelong interest in the sport of target shooting. Berdan's skill with the rifle was such that he had earned a reputation as the nation's top rifle shot during the decade of the 1850's.[4]

Yet once involved in the great industrial revolution sweeping the United States, Berdan's other skills became quickly evident. Employment at Joseph Hall's threshing machine shop in Rochester, New York resulted in a new and innovative design for that equipment, developed by the young engineer. Berdan obtained a patent, moved to Chicago, and was soon engaged in the manufacture of threshing machinery. Then, with the gold craze electrifying the nation, Berdan's fertile mind had turned to California's gold fields. His "Berdan's Gold Quartz Crushing Machine" was patented in the U.S. and in England. During his lengthy travels, New York, London, and California were but a few of the many stops, and while in England he reportedly effected the sale of manufacturing rights for $200,000, a staggering sum in the 1850's.[5]

Wealthy and a man of prominence, Berdan married Mary Kimball, a Long Island girl on December 6, 1854. Thereafter a daughter, Sarah, was born in September, 1855, and the Berdans acquired a stylish home-estate in New York. The best seemed only yet to come, for amid Berdan's exposure to the world and its seemingly archaic methods, there were new inventions. His ocean travels produced a new design of lifeboat. His love of food resulted in "Berdan's Mechanical Bakery," which was sold to such cities as Chicago, Louisville, and St. Louis.[6]

Then came a new opportunity; the Civil War. Berdan, notwithstanding his wealth, young family, and bright civilian prospects, was an early organizer in the war effort. His name soon became nationally known, and ever thereafter synonymous with the special forces fighting unit he brought into being. Despite the long standing conviction that Hiram Berdan was the originator of the idea of a sharpshooter corps, there is some evidence that Caspar Trepp, an ex Swiss officer with Crimean War service, may have first suggested the idea. Switzerland had long utilized such special purpose elements in their army, and to a small cadre of former military men from the old country, it was a practical and proven concept. According to one of Berdan's officers who was involved from the beginning, it was Berdan's fellow New Yorker Trepp who in mid 1861 called for the formation of a sharpshooter unit. Trepp, said his countryman Rudolf Aschmann, offered to organize a sharpshooter corps, if "men of influence" would obtain the required government authority.[7]

Hiram Berdan certainly had the connections and the influence. Regardless of the origin of the concept, Berdan was in Washington, D.C. in mid June, 1861, talking about an elite sharpshooter unit with key members of the administration. The army's aged commanding general, Winfield Scott, through his personal secretary, Schuyler Hamilton, wrote on June 14, 1861 that based upon President Abraham Lincoln's and Secretary of War Simon Cameron's endorsement of a sharpshooter regiment, Berdan's idea was of "great value," and the unit would be "advantageously employed." The next day, June 15th, Berdan was given full authority to raise a regiment of sharpshooters, which was to be mustered in within ninety days and armed and equipped "without expense to the government."[8]

Berdan immediately went to work. Bolstered by flattering comments from officials such as General Winfield Scott, who wrote Schuyler Ha-

Colonel Hiram Berdan, 1st U.S. Sharpshooters, circa 1861 (Michael J. McAfee Coll.)

milton, "was very favorably impressed with you personally," the thirty-six year old colonel set about publicizing and organizing his sharpshooters.

Berdan's concept was, indeed, unique in a variety of ways. His sharpshooters would form a separate and distinctive branch of service under Army command. Rather than recruit the unit from a specific and limited geographic area, he sought to obtain the best marksmen available in the Northern states at large. Accordingly, companies were recruited and furnished by various states, including New York, Michigan, New Hampshire, Vermont, Wisconsin, Minnesota, Pennsylvania, and Maine. Due to Berdan's exacting standards for marksmanship, no recruit was to be accepted who at 200 yards was unable to place ten consecutive shots in a target, the average distance of which was not to exceed 5 inches from the center of the bullseye [total of 50 inches maximum string — ie: within a ten inch circle]. There is some evidence, however, that not all recruits were required to pass this test before being accepted.[9]

Since the colonel lived in the New York region, and had strong ties to his former state, Michigan, Berdan heavily recruited in these areas. Of the ten companies mustered into his regiment, four were from New York and three from Michigan. The New York companies were mustered in first, and Captain Caspar Trepp was given command of Company A, composed mostly of Swiss and Germans whose familiarity with rifle shooting was extensive. One of Co. A's recruits, Rudolph Aschmann, commented how "large crowds" of applicants were attracted to the tryouts. Part of the reason, he surmised, was the novelty of the idea in America (perhaps akin to the modern day prospect of joining the green berets or rangers). Another was the anticipated extra bounty, and a fee of up to $60 paid for each target rifle accepted for the regiment. [10]

With the Bull Run fiasco fresh in mind, by early August, 1861 pressures were beginning to build to get the sharpshooters into active service. In fact, so many men had volunteered to serve as marksmen that in September Berdan was authorized to accept the surplus companies for a second sharpshooter regiment.

Berdan was mustered in as colonel of the 1st U.S. Sharpshooters on August 2, 1861, and his first company (A) on August 20th. By the first week in September the various companies had begun to rendezvous at Camp of Instruction, about a half mile from Washington, D.C. [11]

Hiram Berdan, meanwhile, had become a noted celebrity. Following the extensive publicity generated in recruiting his sharpshooters, the organization was of great interest to curious officials and the public. Berdan's camp was constantly being visited by various dignitaries for demonstrations of shooting marksmanship. Using a heavy barreled match rifle fitted with a telescopic sight Berdan frequently demonstrated his skill to the throng of onlookers, once putting ten consecutive shots within the ten inch ring at 600 yards. Most impressed was the Army's new commander, Major General George B. McClellan, with whom Berdan quickly ingratiated himself. McClellan and President Lincoln were present for a shooting match by special invitation in October, 1861, and both tried their skill with target rifles before Berdan allegedly stole the show with an extraordinary shot. Firing off hand at 600 yards, Berdan is said to have placed a bullet through the right eye of a silhouette target, having first called the shot in the presence of Lincoln. [12]

During this period there seemed to be a certain flair of arrogance about Hiram Berdan, an impression that may have been exaggerated by his rather swaggering appearance. Noticeably balding, and with frizzy side whiskers, at first glance he looked the part of perhaps an upstate banker or a county judge. His bulging eyelids contrasted with dark and deep set eyes, which could flash both sad and menacing. Too, a stern set mouth accentuated his often somber countenance. Generally he was impeccably dressed, and fit well the role of a dapper if rather aloof Federal officer. Even in late 1862, when the facial hair was gone except for a fashionably drooping moustache, his manner and appearance remained that of a stylish and important commander, which is precisely what he perceived himself to be.

Vanity was never far from the surface with Hiram Berdan. His business successes had inflated his self worth, and from years of being deferred to, he had acquired an air of importance well beyond the rank of an army colonel.

Perhaps that is what so rankled the men of his regiment. It was soon evident once in camp that Colonel Berdan was not a military man. His lack of basic army knowledge was said to be an embarrassment to all. Described as often making "a fool of himself with his clumsy demeanor," Berdan wisely had accepted a regular army lieutenant, Frederick Mears, as the Sharpshooters' lieutenant colonel. Mears, who had been with the 9th U.S. Infantry at the beginning of the war, was quickly accepted by the men, wrote one of the recruits, because "he combined expert knowledge with salutary strictness and fatherly solicitude for the men." The word quickly spread that Mears had been assigned to the sharpshooters "to cover up for Berdan's incompetence," said a private. Since Mears would not begrudge the men their occasional whiskey while at leisure, he was idolized by the Swiss company in particular.[13]

As a select body of men picked for special service, a strong spirit of independence was evident in the sharpshooters from the beginning. Those officers who acted the part of a martinet were made the butt of jokes, and were generally despised by the men, remembered a sharpshooter veteran many years later.[14]

Berdan, disliked by many for his arrogance and harsh manner, soon became the victim of several practical jokes. On one occasion, Sergeant F. Rohr of Company A, a jovial Swiss who had a special talent for drawing caricatures, decorated the parade ground with one of his more humorous efforts. On a board or large canvas was drawn a bakery scene, with Lt. Col. Mears in the apron of a baker, and next to him his helper, Captain Trepp. Both were shown taking a tray out of the oven with "Colonel Berdan in full regalia on the baking sheet." Nearby in a basket, and "fresh out of the oven," were various other regimental officers who were not on the most favored list with the men. Over the drawing was the caption: "Freshly Baked Officers Available."

Instead of dealing with the matter with a sense of humor, Berdan, said Rudolph Aschmann, was furious, and started an investigation. Generally quick to take offense at a supposed or implied slight, Berdan became increasingly noted in camp for his temperamental and dictatorial manner. Dissension in the ranks and among the sharpshooter officers soon resulted in a series of difficulties, the effect of which plagued the organization for months to come. [15]

Lieutenant Colonel Frederick Mears resigned in late November, 1861, following an alleged controversy with Berdan. The regiment's major, William S. Rowland, described as a "notoriously incompetent" man who was rarely present in camp, departed the following day. [16]

Then, amid the clamor and outcry of both men and officers for what they had been promised when they signed on, the best rifles in the service — which were being denied by a balky Ordnance Department, Berdan was further embarrassed. He was politically maneuvered into appointing two uncertain figures, an outsider, William Y. W. Ripley of the 1st Vermont, and a potential troublemaking rival, Caspar Trepp, the Swiss company's favorite son, as the field officer replacements. [17]

Berdan at the time was particularly plagued by the "gun question." Of all the issues most important to the sharpshooters and their colonel the matter of selection and procurement of their rifles ranked at the very top. A large number of arms salesmen and manufacturer's agents had descended upon Berdan's camp in an attempt to secure the sharpshooters' order for their weapons. Berdan was injured in the eye during a trial of a prototype Spencer rifle on December 25, 1861 when the base of a defective metallic cartridge separated and spewed burning gasses into his face. But there really was little doubt among the men about which arm to adopt, they wanted the Sharps breechloading military rifle. The highly conservative Ordnance Department under Brigadier General James W. Ripley balked, however, at any change from the standard muzzle loading rifle musket then in service. Berdan had personally contributed to the difficulty in mid July, 1861 when he had written to Ripley seeking the Springfield rifle musket for his regiment. By late October, of course, Berdan had a far different perspective, and was so persistent in his attempt to obtain breechloaders that he irritated a considerable number of congressmen and officials. Due to the Ordnance Department's resistance, the matter became a bitter fought political issue, even with various newspapers reporting on the daily developments. Berdan thus was soon personally involved in considerable controversy. [18]

Having alienated various regular army officers in the Ordnance Department, his list of political enemies seemed to increase with every new effort he made to get the breechloaders. His men, moreover, had become ugly over the matter of their weapons. Two companies, C (Michigan)

Captain Thaddeus P. Mott, ex 3d N.Y. Battery, Colonel Hiram Berdan, Brig. Gen. John W. Davidson, U.S. Vols., with staff, at Fort Lincoln, defenses of Washington, D.C., early Sept. 1862. While the Army of the Potomac prepared to fight at Antietam these officers remained behind. Captain Mott, newly commissioned in the 19th U.S. Infantry, and General Davidson, assigned to the District of St. Louis, were en route to the West. Col. Berdan was on sick leave following his Second Bull Run wound. (Courtesy Vermont Historical Society)

and E (New Hampshire) were the only fully armed units in the regiment, having brought their heavy barreled target rifles with them from home. Once in camp it was learned that the $60 bounty for these rifles was un-authorized and would not be paid. Further, when it appeared the men might not get their promised Sharps rifles, a spirit of revolt swept through the regiment. If the recruiting promises were not to be fulfilled perhaps the men would refuse to leave camp. Berdan later wrote that the sharpshooters were in a virtual state of "mutiny" prior to their active ser-vice in the field. This entire matter caused Berdan to pull all of the strings available, including personally involving the president and the army's commander. Yet five months after the controversy began the matter was still at issue, with Berdan's men steadfastly refusing to accept less than what they had been promised. "This was the reason for our long stay in Washington from where we did not depart until spring," wrote a disgruntled sharpshooter. Indeed, so adamant were Berdan's men about their promised rifles that the 1st U.S.S.S. marched off to the war on March 20, 1862 unarmed except for the target rifle companies. [19]

Although Berdan's conduct in the rifle matter later proved to be somewhat unscrupulous, for he played several options according to the politics of the moment, his often controversial conduct in camp became a lesser source of derision once the unit was in the field.

When the bullets began to fly, it was soon observed that Hiram Berdan was seldom to be found on the firing line. The sharpshooters first went into action near Yorktown, Va. on April 4th and 5th, 1862 during the Peninsular Campaign. By the end of the campaign in early July Berdan's repeated absence during heavy fighting resulted in bitter complaints about him among the sharpshooters. At Mechanicsville on June 26, 1862 Berdan was observed by his acting adjutant, 2d Lieutenant J. Smith Brown, riding around camp listening to the heavy firing in the distance which indicated a battle. When the sharpshooters marched toward the sound of the firing Berdan told Lt. Brown to lead the men into action, saying "I am going back to camp to protect the sick." Berdan was next seen by the men the following morning at breakfast. At Gaines' Mill, June 27th, Berdan was on the front line only long enough to post the men as skirmishers before the firing began. He made a short "speech" to the men, said 1st Lt. Charles W. Seaton, telling them "they would have an excellent opportunity to make a name for the sharpshooters that day — for the enemy would probably come over the [open] field in front and every Rebel killed in that field would known to be killed by the sharpshooters." Then Berdan rode away to the rear. That was the last the men on the firing line saw of him until the battle was over. During the heavy fire fight of that day Private Edward D. Trusk, Co. F, who had been detached to guard the knapsacks in the rear, saw Berdan riding about aimlessly, going to the hospital, then coming over to give Trusk some trivial orders. The fighting had gone poorly for the Federals, and about 6 p.m. the broken battle lines resulted in a wild and panicky stream of fugitives and stragglers pouring to the rear. On the firing line, Lieutenant Colonel William Y.W. Ripley, who had taken command of the sharpshooter detachment, was found to be sweat soaked and almost delirious by Lt. Seaton. Fearing sunstroke, Seaton gave Ripley a drink of whiskey and rode with him to the rear. A half mile down the road they encountered Colonel Berdan. Berdan said he had been after ammunition for the men, and told Seaton to go back to his company, that he would assist Lt. Col. Ripley to the hospital. [20]

Standing nearby at the time was Corporal Cassius Peck of Company F, on detached quartermaster's duty. Berdan asked Ripley all manner of questions, said Peck, about how the men had behaved, what was occurring at the front, etc., when a horde of stragglers burst over a nearby hill. Behind them was the sound of the enemy shouting as they charged forward — so it was supposed. Berdan turned to Ripley and said: "we must get out of this, it is no place for us." Helping Ripley on his horse, Berdan led the way to the rear, and held the lieutenant colonel by the arm to keep him from falling from the saddle. By now "the stragglers were going by us fast," said Corporal Peck, who was riding the Quartermaster's horse. Ripley, although reeling with dizziness, said to Berdan that something must be done to rally the men. Farther along, Ripley became adamant, "For God's sake, let go of me and try and rally these men," he told Berdan. Finally, when they were beyond a nearby hill, Berdan turned Ripley over to Peck's care, and remained behind. Ripley's parting words to his colonel were: "Had you not better go see to the men, there is no one in charge of them." Berdan only replied: "leave them to the captains," — he had no idea of where to find them. [21]

Berdan's own version of what happened next was bombastically worded in his official report: "[I saw] not less than 12,000 of our men and officers, each apparently making quick time for the bridge [over the Chickahominy River]....Seeing no effort made to rally the men I rode through them to the right and left, appealing to the officers to get the men together, and I would go down to the bridge and bring up the rear. The bridge was full when I reached it, and finding my appeals to the officers and men of no avail, I drew my pistol and threatened to shoot the first officer or man who passed me; and finding these threats of no use, I fired several shots over their heads before I succeeded in checking the rush, which had become almost a panic." [22]

Over emphasizing his own role, and extolling the utility of his sharpshooters on the battlefield was a technique that Berdan had perfected to previous advantage in his reports of earlier actions. On this occasion it didn't work. Brigadier General George W. Morell, his division commander, gruffly endorsed on Berdan's report: "Colonel Berdan was not in the fight at Gaines' Mill. What occurred far to the rear near the bridge I do not know of my own knowledge, but I have every reason to believe this statement highly exaggerated."

Indeed, Corporal Paul M. Thompson of the sharpshooters found Berdan at sundown on the 27th "riding around on horseback" not particularly involved in anything, but said he was located behind the first two lines of rallied men.[23]

Again, on July 1st at Malvern Hill, Berdan's conduct fell into a familiar pattern. Lieutenant Seaton said the colonel sent the sharpshooters into action from well in the rear, saying: "scatter out — scatter out there men, double quick, and go till you meet the enemy." Once the fighting had begun, Berdan was no where to be seen. His acting adjutant, Lieutenant Brown, found him well to the rear when sent on an errand. Berdan explained that he had been getting fresh meat for the men whom he knew would be tired and hungry. Using the difficulty of the men finding this food as a pretext, Berdan then went to rear another mile or two, allegedly to bring it forward.[24]

Berdan's conduct while in a combat situation became so criticized among his men that he seemed compelled to constantly make reference to his alleged exposure to danger at every opportunity. On the Peninsula he had written: "As for myself I feel amply repaid for the danger I ran in reconnoitering the ground under fire, posting the men, encouraging and directing them through the day, by the confident feeling that we must have killed and wounded several hundred rebels...." Ranking generals such as Major General Fitz John Porter had complimented Berdan's unit highly, praising them for efficiency and effectiveness. Thereby, Berdan basked in the glory of the sharpshooter's reputation, adopting it much as his own.[25]

His men were not fooled by such bombast. The regimental historian, long after the war wrote with intense feeling that "the real test [of an officer] was on the field of battle; if the officers stayed with their men, their respect was honorably earned. If they tried to keep out and away from the line of danger, it was deservedly lost."[26]

Berdan, already talked about among the men for his "cowardice" in the presence of the enemy, ran into further trouble once the fighting shifted to the line of the Rappahannock in Virgina. At Bull Run II, August 30, 1862, Berdan put up a brave front, for a short while.

Leading the ten companies of sharpshooters forward to the skirmish line, Colonel Berdan halted in a clover field, "just out of musket range of a woods in which the enemy were supposed to be." He then sent Lieutenant William Nash forward with ten men into the woods to see if the enemy was there. When Nash and his men found a heavy line of gray infantry beyond the woods near a road, Berdan sent Major George G. Hastings forward with the sharpshooters deployed as skirmishers. Apparently, Berdan rode with them behind the line. When skirmish firing began along the road, remembered Corporal Cassius Peck, a bullet came very near the colonel. Berdan called for volunteers to go and root out the enemy, then promptly went to the rear, saying he was going to see one of the generals. Indeed, Brigadier General Daniel Butterfield said that Berdan came to him and reported a large force of the enemy present in his front. Butterfield sent Berdan back to remain with his regiment, saying that if he had further communications to send an orderly.

Later, once the heavy fighting had begun, Butterfield sent two or three aides to find Berdan and have him push forward his men. The aides couldn't find him. Berdan's aide de camp, Lieutenant Brown, said Berdan never did return to the firing line. A corporal, sent to the rear for ammunition, found Berdan a half or three quarters of a mile behind the front line. Meanwhile, his regiment had moved too far to the right, and Butterfield had to replace Berdan's skirmishers with another unit. Another regimental commander complained that Berdan's sharpshooters were out of position, being much closer to the main battle line than they should have been.[27]

Ironically, Berdan, again in the rear during the fighting, came away a casualty. While riding about a stray shell exploded nearby, and a fragment struck Berdan in the left chest. The wound produced a severe contusion, and apparently some bleeding, but he was later described as only slightly wounded. It was evidently just the sort of injury that Berdan could magnify into an extended absence and some popular acclaim.

For the next three and a half months Berdan languished at Washington, complaining of severe pain, spitting of blood, and weakness from a loss of blood, although he regretted "more than words can express that I am compelled to be away from my regiment." Despite this "wound" Berdan was able to father a daughter while on sick leave.[28]

Moreover, his "wholly unfit" physical status didn't keep Berdan from writing and surreptitiously publishing a highly inflated account of Bull Run II. In order to cover up his direct involvement in giving his report to a reporter for the New York Times, Berdan concocted a story that his adjutant had fallen asleep while permitting the reporter to copy down the list of casualties, and the reporter had thus copied the entire report. His adjutant later testified that he saw Berdan give the report to the New York Times reporter, and watched him copy it. When Berdan wanted the adjutant to sign a statement about giving the reporter the report and falling asleep, the lieutenant refused and soon transferred to another regiment.

Soon the sharpshooters were ordered to march in pursuit of Lee during the Antietam Campaign, but Berdan stayed behind in Washington, D.C. Captain John B. Isler said that the colonel told him he was staying behind to collect Sharps rifles belonging to the regiment. Accordingly, Berdan missed the bloodiest day of the war, September 17, 1862. [29]

By now many of the sharpshooter's officers had more than enough of Berdan's antics. On October 6th, said a senior officer, charges were filed against Colonel Berdan for misbehavior before the enemy and conduct unbecoming an officer.

The major sources of his trouble within the regiment, Berdan had learned, were Lieutenant Colonel Trepp, Major Hastings, and Captain William W. Winthrop. Of all the troublemakers in the regiment, Caspar Trepp, the ex Swiss professional, was the most threatening. Trepp was a no-nonsense commander, brave to a fault, and a strict disciplinarian, but well liked and respected by the men who knew they could count on him in a fight. He had been on leave of absence for sickness from September 9, 1862 but had returned to duty and command of the regiment in early October. Trepp reported the 1st U.S. Sharpshooters in good condition and well disciplined when he mustered the unit for pay on November 1st. Berdan, still in Washington, wanted the payrolls forwarded to him for his personal approval. Trepp, however, refused to comply, writing to the staff officer involved that Berdan, until he was present, had no authority over the matter. Berdan, who saw the note in early December, endorsed it with a caustic remark about a lack of proper spirit. [30]

The Battle of Fredricksburg having been fought on December 12th and 13th, Berdan suddenly felt well enough to rejoin his command on December 17, 1862. Almost immediately there occurred a confrontation of a "violent nature" between Berdan and Trepp, said a fellow officer. On December 19, 1862 the reviewing officer for the 5th Corps, Lieutenant Colonel Nelson B. Bartram of the 17th New York Infantry, found the 1st Sharpshooters deficient in a wide variety of criteria. Indifferent appearance, lax discipline, poor skill in the manual of arms, missing bayonets, dirty accouterments, and improperly instructed guards, were but a few of the many negative evaluations. Bartram then proceeded in his summary to chastise the regiment in the strongest terms:

The regiment presents an exceedingly unmilitary appearance; the men are not 'set up' — are perfect slouches and slovens in appearance and hardly any two are uniformed alike. About half the men are without bayonets. I found upon inquiry that the men were allowed to chose whether they would or would not take them. Indeed, this system seemed to attain throughout, as the Quarter Master informed me that he could have obtained U.S. uniforms, but that the men would not have them. Colonel Berdan, who has just rejoined the Regt. after a long absence on sick leave informed me that he has obtained new uniforms and equipments needed, such as bayonets, etc, and that a reformation speedy and thorough will take place. The Regimental camp is very irregular and badly situated.

Highly sensitive about his reputation, Berdan explained that the majority of his officers were indifferent, implying that they were to blame. In fact, when he finally saw Bartram's damning report just before Christmas, he hastily appended a self serving explanation. Said Berdan: "...the report is quite as favorable as I could expect, considering the deplorable state I found my Regt. in. The uncertainty of the success of a Regt. of Sharp Shooters brought to me a very poor class of applicants for commissions. Add to this six months demoralization on the gun question in camp; also the fact that the reg't was taken into the field in a state of mutiny on the gun question, and forced there to take such guns as I could get until the Sharps Rifles was done; also the demoralization consequent to detached service by single co's, and some idea may be formed of the importance of my presence with the Regt. and the constant work necessary for me to make over the worthless officers to make the Regt. of any value to the service. But for this I would not be here with a leave of absence in my pocket [unexpired] against the advice of the Surgeon General and Surgeon Clymer."[31]

Privately, Berdan was fuming over the matter. Immediately there were reports in the regiment of strict disciplinary measures. "The boys are blacking their belts & boots." wrote a sharpshooter. "Old Berdan makes the men slick up." The day after Christmas he summoned Lieutenant Colonel Trepp to his headquarters tent and ordered him, along with Major Hastings, "to take a rifle and go out and drill in the manual of arms under the instruction of 1st Lieutenant Nash." Trepp and Hastings obeyed the order, but were later overheard by Berdan cursing and complaining about their treatment as he walked by Trepp's tent. Berdan entered and confronted Trepp, demanding an apology. Trepp adamantly refused, and in a long letter of complaint to Berdan tendered his immediate resignation, stating: "I decline therefore to apologize for having complained in indignant terms at what I consider a humiliation put on me by you."[32]

Berdan later alleged the order was only a "request," and seems to have had orders drawn up stating that such was the case. As for Trepp's resignation, Berdan had another course of action in mind — a court martial. On January 25, 1863 Trepp was arrested and confined to camp, pending his trial. The charges mirrored the old complaint against Berdan, which was as yet unsettled: misbehavior before the enemy. Tacked on were additional charges, including insubordination and absence without leave. When Trepp appealed to be allowed to leave camp in order to visit other regiments so as to obtain evidence for his defense, Berdan disapproved the request.[33]

With Trepp, Hastings, and Captain Winthrop in arrest, matters seemed to brighten considerably for Colonel Berdan during the early winter of 1863. On January 14th Berdan was appointed "chief of sharpshooters" by the army's commander, Major General Ambrose Burnside. As such both regiments of sharpshooters were placed under Berdan's command, to be "a distinct arm of the service" and report directly to Burnside's headquarters. Accordingly, Berdan's spirits had soared to such an extent that he participated at the time in the sharpshooters' carnival, beating the entire regiment in long jumping, perhaps a rather remarkable recovery for one so long disabled.[34]

When Trepp and the others were easily acquitted during late February, Berdan was counter charged by Trepp for tampering with a witness prior to the lieutenant colonel's proceedings. Berdan thus had to face trial in early March on this and the original charges.

Although Berdan protested, saying he was "not accountable or responsible to my inferiors for my absence" on any occasion, the trial proceeded to a controversial ending.

After being excused by the court from having to present any evidence on his behalf, Berdan was judged "not guilty" on all counts. The reviewing officer, Brigadier General A. W. Whipple, was incensed by the court's "error." He wrote that at least three and portions of a fourth specification regarding Berdan's misbehavior before the enemy had been "clearly proved." "A commanding officer is expected to be with his troops, especially upon the field of battle and during an engagement," said Whipple, and such "prima facie evidence of [Berdan's] misbehavior or at least neglect of duty" as had been given in testimony was valid. Although the court's error was "greatly to be regretted," said Whipple, Berdan would not be made to suffer as a result, and he was released from arrest. Even following the second trial, held immediately after the first, on charges of Berdan's tampering with a witness, Brigadier General Whipple said that again the court erred in acquitting the sharpshooter colonel. Testimony "clearly proved" that Berdan had suggested to two of his subordinates that they should testify in a certain manner or they might be court martialed for giving false evidence. These acts were "highly improper," said Whipple, and he disapproved the proceedings.[35]

Having been most fortunate with these trials, Berdan had another favorable break when any further action on the matter was dropped due to the approach of the spring campaign. Berdan refused to forget what had transpired, however, and said a witness who had testified against him, "from then on [he] took every opportunity to make life unpleasant for me." Fortunately, for all, an uneasy truce of sorts occurred between Trepp and Berdan, for by the end of the trial Berdan was called to brigade command, and Trepp assumed command of the regiment under Berdan.[36]

At the Battle of Chancellorsville in early May the Sharpshooters played a conspicuous part and earned considerable laurels. Near Catherine Furnace on May 2d the 1st Sharpshooters surrounded and captured 365 officers and men of the 23d Georgia. On May 3d, the sharpshooters held the center of the 3d Corps line, earning high praise from Major General Dan Sickles.

During the furious fighting of that day Major George Hastings was wounded. On his way to the hospital he found Col. Berdan in the customary place, well in the rear, near some pack mules. No one had seen him on the firing line after the fighting had begun, and Hastings, obviously disgusted, wrote to Trepp from New York several weeks later: "I authorize you to sign my name to any proper paper signed by yourself and others, addressed to the president recommending against Hiram Berdan's promotion, or against his having control of more sharpshooters."[see Major George Hastings' report - Appendix B]

Trepp, who was again angry about Berdan's behavior, had written to a friend in the adjutant general's office about another court martial of the colonel. His friend advised him it would be best not to press charges, but to send an account of Berdan's role at Chancellorsville to Secretary of War Edwin Stanton, signed by the sharpshooter officers. Trepp, for his part, had acted with conspicuous bravery in bringing forward reinforcements at a critical moment, but was snubbed by Berdan, who refused to acknowledge the deed or even mention Trepp in his official report.[37]

Although Berdan found ready cause to be absent on leave during much of June — his second child, a daughter, Elizabeth, was born on June 15th — the die was cast with regard to close scrutiny of Berdan's conduct during future actions. Berdan appears to have been well aware of the intensifying pressure, and during the Gettysburg Campaign seemed to be looking for the right opportunity to silence his critics.

The opportunity came amid one of the most controversial aspects of the entire battle. On July 2d the 3d Corps commander, Dan Sickles, determined to move forward and occupy a line farther advanced than the Cemetery Ridge main battle line. Since the 3d Corps anchored the extreme left flank of the Army of the Potomac, it was a critical maneuver, designed so Sickles said, to take advantage of the higher ground near the Emmitsburg Road. Despite considerable confusion about the movement after the war, Sickles apparently moved forward in apprehension of an enemy attack, intending to avoid another fiasco such as had occurred at Chancellorsville where Sickles' position on high ground at Hazel Grove had been abandoned. This had allowed the Confederates to move artillery to the spot, which later helped make the Chancellor House area untenable.[38]

The specific rationale for the move, Sickles later claimed, had come from a reconnaissance led by Colonel Hiram Berdan, which discovered the enemy threatening his front.[39]

Berdan's reconnaissance was later the basis for much self inflating propaganda by the colonel, who implied he had risked his life in order to buy time for the army to advance and fight Longstreet's flank attack.

The actual circumstances and motives when examined from contemporary evidence provides a far different perspective. A 100 man detachment of Berdan's 1st U.S. Sharpshooters had been deployed near the Rogers house along the Emmitsburg Road since mid morning on July 2d, skirmishing with Confederates in the vicinity of Spangler's Woods. Brigadier General David Birney, Sickles' 1st Division commander, had become concerned about the volume of this skirmish firing, said to be "constant," coming from his front. About noon he sent to Sickles for permission to send a patrol into the woods farther to the left to see what troops the enemy had present, and discover any threatening movement. Sickles knew that the army's commander Major General George G. Meade was awaiting developments, not knowing whether to take offensive or defensive action pending the location of the enemy's exact positions. Without hesitation, Sickles approved the reconnaissance.

Birney selected for the work another 100 man detachment of the 1st U.S. Sharpshooters, and for their support, the 3d Maine Infantry, 214 officers and men under Colonel Moses B. Lakeman. Colonel Berdan was to have overall command of the patrol, with Lieutenant Colonel Caspar Trepp serving as commander of the detachment of 1st Sharpshooters (Companies D,E,F,I).

Berdan, for once, was under close official observation, as Captain Joseph C. Briscoe, General Birney's aide, had been told by Birney to ride along. Berdan marched the patrol south along the Emmitsburg Road past the Peach Orchard, then west and along a narrow residential road that led to the schoolhouse near Willoughby Run. When adjacent to the length of woods that ran nearly northwest to Pitzer's Run a skirmish line consisting of the four companies of sharpshooters under Trepp was deployed into the timber. Lakeman's 3d Maine was halted a short distance behind, along the Emmitsburg Road. As the troops deployed a young boy who lived in a farmhouse at the site warned Berdan's men, "Look out! there are lots of rebels in there [pointing to the woods], in rows." The sharpshooters scoffed at the lad, and about noon or shortly thereafter, Berdan's skirmish line followed by the 3d Maine pushed forward through the thick woods in a northwesterly direction.[40]

Meanwhile, Confederate skirmishers in the vicinity of the Spangler Woods undoubtedly had seen Berdan's patrol march along the Emmitsburg Road and enter Pitzer's Woods. "As we marched the enemy must have seen every man from the time we reached the [Emmitsburg] road until we entered the woods," later reflected the thoroughly disgusted Caspar Trepp. "All this time we were marching or halting in plain view of the enemy. For this violation of rules of secret expeditions we paid dearly...."[41]

It so happened that Berdan's patrol at the moment was beyond the extreme right flank of the Confederate Army, which was formed in Spangler's Woods near Pitzer Run. These Confederates were the all Alabama brigade of Brigadier General Cadmus M. Wilcox, in Major General Richard H. Anderson's division, of Lieutenant General A. P. Hill's corps. Wilcox had been shuffled about that morning, being redeployed after having guarded the far right on detached duty during the evening of July 1st. After rejoining the division in mid morning, Wilcox had been sent through Spangler's Woods to confront the line of Federal skirmishers along the Emmitsburg Road north of the Peach Orchard.

Because Pitzer's Woods on Wilcox's right had been unoccupied by the Confederates, once sightings of Berdan's patrol were evidently reported, Wilcox sought to push a line of skirmishers into the woods "not knowing whether the woods...was [now] occupied by the enemy." Skirmishers from the 10th Alabama Infantry went forward into the woods, while the remainder of that regiment and the 11th Alabama prepared to support them. The 10th Alabama evidently went around the edge of the woods, but the 11th Alabama marched into the open meadow between Spangler's and Pitzer's Woods. [42]

Caspar Trepp wrote that the sharpshooters had not gone very far into the woods when firing erupted between the two lines of skirmishers. The Federals outnumbered the Alabamians, and armed with their Sharps breechloaders, they easily pushed the Confederates back though the woods on the run. When the right elements of Trepp's line came to the edge of the timber, which slanted obliquely to their left, in the open meadow they saw the 11th Alabama, moving toward a fence line some 300 yards beyond Spangler's Woods. Immediately the sharpshooters opened with an accurate rifle fire. Berdan, who said he could see three columns in motion beyond the woods, gave the order for Lakeman's 3d Maine to come up on the double quick. By the time Lakeman and his troops arrived the sharpshooters were under a heavy fire from both the 10th Alabama, moving through the woods from the northwest, and the 11th Alabama, firing from behind a rail fence in the open field. Lakeman was chagrined to find that the sharpshooters had taken cover behind most of the trees, so that his men were generally in the open and "filled the intervals." The result was a heavy loss in the 3d Maine of 48 in killed, wounded, and missing in the span of about fifteen minutes. The sharpshooters lost heavily also; 2 officers wounded and 16 enlisted casualties.

Finally, the colonel of the 10th Alabama led a charge and Berdan gave the order to fall back firing. The 10th Alabama pursued only a short distance, and Berdan's patrol reformed on the Emmitsburg Road and promptly returned to the Federal lines.

The encounter had lasted no more than twenty minutes, but Trepp found that his men had fired their Sharps so frequently that they had only about 5 rounds of ammunition remaining per man (despite this the Confederates seemed to have suffered slightly fewer casualties — the 10th Alabama reported a loss of 10 killed and 28 wounded in the fight, and the 11th Alabama 1 officer and 17 men wounded). [43]

Berdan reported to Birney about 2 p.m. that "three columns of the enemy's forces" were marching to the Federal left, and he had been driven back by "overwhelming numbers." "This important information," said Birney was promptly given to Sickles, who immediately ordered Birney forward to the high ground at the Peach Orchard. Sickles had been worried about an attack on his front, and General Meade and the others had chosen to pay little attention to his situation. Accordingly, Sickles had decided to act on his own. At about 3 p.m. Sickles' entire corps advanced to the Emmitsburg Road line, creating a dangerous exposure of the Army of the Potomac's left flank. Sickles' unauthorized move created a gap in the army's main defensive line on Cemetery Ridge, and exposed the key to the battlefield, Little Round Top, to the enemy's assault.

Indeed, Major General Meade had ridden over to see Sickles while the movement was in progress. According to Meade, he was in the act of remonstrating with Sickles about the impropriety of this movement when the very worst happened. "I was explaining to him that he was too far in advance, and discussing with him the propriety of withdrawing, when the enemy opened on him with several batteries in his front and on his flank, and immediately brought forward columns of infantry...."

It was Longstreet's famous flank attack which came within an eyelash of a stunning success. Sickles, Meade, and perhaps the entire army were tottering on the brink of an enormous disaster. Ironically, they were saved by somewhat of a fluke. The 6th Corps had only recently arrived about 2 p.m. after a forced march of thirty two miles in fifteen hours. Posting these exhausted troops as a reserve on the right, Meade had ordered the 5th Corps, which had been the reserve at that point, to prepare to move to the army's left flank if needed. The 5th Corps was thus able to rush forward and secure the left flank, including Little Round Top, by the narrowest of margins. [44]

Sickles, who lost a leg to a cannon ball shortly after the fighting began that afternoon, later initiated a bitter controversy with Meade and others over his forward movement, claiming it had disrupted the enemy's plans and had proved to be the army's saving grace. Hiram Berdan was only too happy to further Sickles' cause, claiming after the war that it was his sharpshooters' reconnaissance which had not only discovered the threatening enemy columns, but had delayed the enemy so as to allow "time to strengthen our left." Berdan further claimed high personal honors during the patrol, stating he had risked his life in the critical moment before the firing began, sitting alone on horseback well in advance of his line, scouting the enemy's position while waiting for Birney's aide to escape to safety. Speaking at a veterans' reunion twenty six years later Berdan postured about his bravery: "This would be sure death to me," he had thought, stating that a Confederate officer had singled him out, saying to his men not to fire unless fired upon, but if the fighting began to shoot that officer. Still, Berdan had resolutely given the order, "Follow me, advance firing."[45]

Berdan's entire account seems to have been mostly a fabrication. He had not discovered the advancing Confederates, nor had his men delayed Longstreet's attack. The troops his patrol encountered were not Longstreet's men, they were A.P. Hill's, long present in the area. Their role was merely to act as supports for the flank attack which would originate farther south. Longstreet's men, on their circuitous march to the extreme left flank of the Federal army, did not appear in the vicinity until about 3:30 p.m.

Moreover, Berdan's conducting of the reconnaissance was faulty, as Trepp had quickly pointed out. "This detachment might have been marched from the original position to a point where the engagement took place perfectly concealed from view of the enemy and without loss of time," said Trepp in reflecting upon the sharpshooters' costly confrontation with the Alabamians.

Berdan, who apparently rode with Birney's aide a short distance into Pitzer's woods for a brief look prior to sending forward the sharpshooters, evidently did not penetrate the timber in any great depth. A member of Company E who was present said Berdan was gone only a short time before returning. Firing is reported to have begun spontaneously between the sharpshooters and the 10th Alabama's skirmishers only after the Federal line advanced partially through Pitzer's woods.[46]

Further, based upon the tactical situation, Berdan's personal behavior during the affair is subject to question. In view of his previous behavior it is easy to picture the sharpshooter colonel safely positioned behind one of the larger trees once the fighting began. His observation that three columns of troops were moving against his men only confirmed how far back he must have been positioned in order to confuse the 10th and 11th Alabama for such "overwhelming numbers." When attacked by the 10th Alabama alone, Berdan promptly gave the order to fall back, said Trepp, who reported that at the time they had been maintaining their position for about ten minutes.[47]

Whatever the exact circumstances following Gettysburg, Hiram Berdan had had enough of the Army. On August 7th the 38 year old colonel secured a leave of absence and took his departure, never to return. As yet only a colonel, with much of his regiment against him (there was the prospect of a further inquiry or court martial), and evidencing a strong dislike for combat situations, Berdan's thoughts began to turn to a more promising line of endeavor. Already he had experiments underway for a new system of breechloading rifles which would incorporate the superior accuracy of the Whitworth rifle's hexagonal bore. Perhaps envisioning enormous profits on an Army contract for such a system, Berdan remained in New York much of the time developing the prototypes. Meanwhile, he repeatedly obtained extended leaves of absence from the Army because of "disability." Although his old regimental antagonist Caspar Trepp was killed at Mine Run on November 30th, Berdan had few thoughts of returning to the sharpshooters. He submitted his resignation late in 1863, and was mustered out of the service January 2, 1864.[48]

Little more than a month later Berdan was corresponding with the Chief of Ordnance about his new breechloader, while casually including mention of his "wound." Although Hiram Berdan was not successful in selling the Army this or subsequent breechloading rifle systems of his design, he had at last returned to his special calling. His inventive genius produced an almost endless series of small arms improvements. Working with Remington, Colt, Lamson (Windsor Manufacturing Co.) and others, a series of new model arms, conversions, and parts of his design (such as the extractor used on the U.S. Model 1868 rifle) were utilized to a varying extent during the next decade.

Of special importance was Berdan's famous external primer system for center fire metallic cartridges, patented in 1866, which proved highly successful and became widely used. A unique mechanical fuze for artillery shells, designed to detonate after a preselected number of revolutions, also was Berdan's invention. Most important as a financial success was Berdan's design of a new rifle for the Russians — the Berdan Type I (and later Type II) Rifle. Berdan went to Russia to help establish the Tula Arsenal in 1869, and remained in Europe for a number of years. When he returned to live in the United States about 1886 Berdan's honored place in the history of small arms development was assured. [49]

As an ex military man Berdan obviously took great pride in the post war brevet of brigadier general (for Chancellorsville), despite a similar brevet of major general (for Gettysburg) which failed confirmation in the Senate. Most important to Berdan in the twilight of his life, however, was his pioneering effort in implementing and proving breechloading rifles as a superior system for the military. With Berdan's flair for the dramatic he had spread word of his sharpshooters' effectiveness wherever he had traveled. "You are as well known among military men in Europe as you are in this country," he had told a reunion of the sharpshooters in 1888, "and you are regarded as the men who taught the world the superiority of breechloaders over muzzleloaders." [50]

Part genius, part charlatan, and both a success and a failure in his military endeavors, Hiram Berdan died suddenly of a heart attack while at the Metropolitan Club in Washington, D.C. on March 31, 1893. His epitaph was perhaps best written some years earlier by one of the men who knew him best, a former sharpshooter lieutenant. He had thoughtfully appraised Berdan's war time contribution and recorded what seems to be the fairest assessment: great honor was due to Hiram Berdan for organizing and arming the sharpshooters, but equal if not greater consideration was due to the other officers for the unit's enormous fighting reputation. [51]

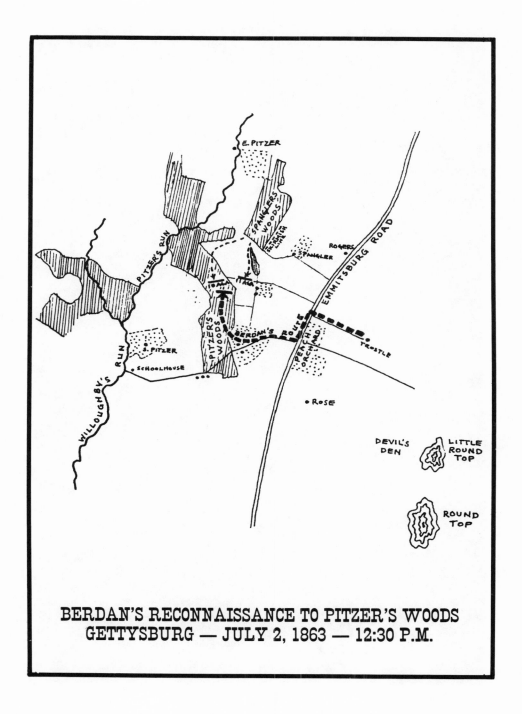

**BERDAN'S RECONNAISSANCE TO PITZER'S WOODS
GETTYSBURG — JULY 2, 1863 — 12:30 P.M.**

PART II:
BERDAN'S SHARPSHOOTERS —
THE MEN

Fighting was what the recruits joining Berdan's sharpshooters had enlisted to do. Yet little were they aware of the ordeal involved in military life, even for such a unique group of skilled marksmen.

The recruiting broadsides had advertised for the best of men, promoting an elitist organization. An advertisement in the Faribault, Minnesota Central Republican for December 11, 1861 decreed:

All able bodied men used to the rifle, or having a good eye & nerve, who desire to join this branch of the army, will be examined at St. Paul; or all able bodied men who bring a certificate from a J.[ustice of the] P.[eace] or other county official, that they have made a string of 50 inches in 10 consecutive shots at 200 yards, with globe or telescope sights from a rest, will be mustered into the pay & service of the U.S., & furnished subsistence & comfortable quarters, at the Snelling House, St. Paul, as soon as they present themselves. Will use Sharps improved Breech Loading Rifle.[52]

Rudolph Aschmann, later an officer, wrote how eager the 106 men forming Company A were for war service, and how there was such a rush of volunteers that many would be sharpshooters had to be turned away from the organization. The recruiting promises of favorable pay, bounty, special service, and anticipation of a grand adventure had everyone high with enthusiasm. Even a year later the sharpshooter service was heralded as a "passport to glory."[53]

Qualifying trials for sharpshooters had been held throughout Michigan in July, 1861, and from the reports of the newspapers apparently about half the applicants passed the test. At Grand Rapids, Michigan on

---

A well equipped sharpshooter, Chauncey B. Maltby, Co. B, 2d U.S.S.S., from the pre active service period of Feb./March, 1862. Note the leather leggings and the contrast in the green frock coat and sky blue pants. A black ostrich feather is affixed to his kepi. The Colt revolving rifle musket shows the bright finish which the men considered "pretty to look at." (Michael J. McAfee Coll.)

July 16th ten candidates competed and five were accepted with shot strings that measured 33 3/8" to 44 5/8". Hiram Berdan conducted trials throughout the summer at Weehawken, N.J., and even borrowed "a Swiss Rifle" for testing recruits that August, which as of two years later had not been returned. Actually, some of the companies seem to have had less exacting standards for enlistment than the stated marksmanship criteria. A captain recruiting a company in Minnesota wrote that even those men not skilled with the rifle might be induced to join, since with training they might be brought to proficiency within a few days. "Let no good man stay behind because he is not used to the rifle," urged the captain in private correspondence. Most of the men who enlisted as sharpshooters were probably a little older than their volunteer infantry counterparts, averaging 24-1/2 years of age in Company D, and 26 years old in Company G.[54]

In the beginning there was little to dispel the initial euphoria of the men at their enlistment. Some recruits from Company B of the 2d Sharpshooters got a pass to leave camp and went frolicking "crosslot through the woods, full of sport, feeling like colts let loose." In the New York companies the early recruits found camp at Weehawken highly to their liking — there were meals provided by an innkeeper, "many a pleasant hour with beer and other spirits" at a nearby tavern, and passes to visit New York. Indeed, army life seemed almost pleasant.

Disillusionment was not long in coming. Once on hand at Camp of Instruction, near Washington, D.C., the abrupt perspective of military reality for each recruit was only too soon understood. Not only were the government's "promises" of higher pay, extra bounty, and superior weapons unfulfilled, but their former civilian freedom was at an end.[55]

The 1st Sharpshooters, especially, included some highly independent and obstreperous characters. Very few of the men knew each other at the beginning of their service, having been recruited from different locations. Being without formal military instruction, many of the men knew how to shoot, but little else. One strapping recruit from Company F managed to get himself into trouble while on guard duty. Sitting on a fence rail, his bayoneted musket thrust into the ground, he summoned an approaching field grade officer from Washington by shouting, "I say! Come over here a moment." When berated by the officer for unmilitary conduct, the recruit was incensed, saying he merely wanted some tobacco, — "to take a friendly chew."

Like many volunteer units the men were fun loving, and always looking for good humor amid their often dreary routine of drill, inspection, fatigue, camp, and guard duty. They joked about the initials "U.S.S.S." embroidered on many of their caps, it stood for "Uncle Sam's Sorry Soldiers" they said. Fun was poked at the white pantaloons often worn by their major to impress his lady friends. In a more practical matter, to the chagrin of the enlisted men of Company A their supply of liquor was cut off, forcing one enterprising individual to resort to smuggling alcoholic beverages into camp in milk cans. [56]

Yet what rankled the men the most was what they considered petty treatment at the hands of bureaucrats and ranking officers. Beyond the serious small arms issue, there was the matter of food peddlers being banned from camp, and the difficulty of getting a pass. One enterprising corporal, in order to take part in an impromptu "chicken shoot," forged a pass and won the contest, much to the complaint of those with legitimate passes.

If the sharpshooters delighted in their spirit of independence, it was at a certain price. Indeed, the entire regiment seemed to have earned somewhat of a roughneck reputation during their six months stay in the Washington, D.C. area. When fuel for camp fires was sought, often the nearest wood was appropriated, including apparently the board fence of Glenwood Cemetery, adjacent to the sharpshooters' camp. Many complaints were registered by outsiders over the matter, and when the men left camp, but little of the cemetery fence remained standing, said a smug sharpshooter. [57]

Known familiarly as the "Green Coats," due to their distinctive dark green uniform coats, both sharpshooter regiments cut a rather swashbuckling appearance on the parade ground. In addition to the green coats, light blue trousers, kepis with a black plume, and leather leggings completed their basic apparel.

Despite the attention given to the organization in the newspapers, and their popularity during Saturday target practice demonstrations, difficulty with government officials and even disputes with prospective companies of recruits were noted. One company that had intended to join the sharpshooters did not like Berdan upon their arrival, said a Wisconsin private, so they joined another unit. We have been "humbugged" [deceived] again he wrote, adding that he feared a worse continuation of such by Berdan. [58]

During the long winter months in camp near Washington the sharpshooters arduously practiced skirmish drill, learning to obey bugle

commands while deployed, and to scale obstructions, including a neighbor's private fence. The mood of the men was generally good, but camping in the mud and rain had taken its toll in sickness. Measles were particularly prevalent, and small pox was among the various communicable diseases spread through the network of Army camps. The men of Company A, the Swiss and Germans, were healthier than the other companies, due so they said to boiling their meats and dining on a fare of soups and vegetables, rather than frying their foods.[59]

By far the favorite pastime was target shooting, a sport that the sharpshooters maintained when time permitted throughout the term of their service. Just how good these sharpshooters were as marksmen was demonstrated repeatedly during matches for prizes that sometimes amounted to $150.00 total purse. A two shot string of 4-1/4" at 220 yards barely won for Vermonter Ai Brown of Company F on Thanksgiving Day, 1861. Berdan's own mark was 5-9/16," firing off hand. Since only Companies C,E, and a portion of F had target rifles, the remaining companies, which were unarmed awaiting government weapons, were merely onlookers.[60]

Little more than a year later, following actual service in the field, the sharpshooters held target practice with most companies participating, using the open sighted Sharps breechloading rifle with set triggers. In winter camp near Falmouth, Va. on January 13 and 14, 1863, eight companies, C,D,E,F,G,H,I,and K, fired in inter company competition. On the 14th the variable winds were described as strong, the day cloudy, and the men fired across a deep ravine at board targets. The results were as follows:[61]

	Distance	Target Size	Shots Fired	Hits	Measurement
Company C	unrecorded	unrecorded	70	37	11-31/32"
Company D	200 yds.	3'1" x 2'1"	42	21	11-3/4"
Company E	200 yds.	23" x 26"	16	5	10-2/5"
Company F	180 yds.	5' x 4'	79	76	13-17/19"
Company G	250 yds.	2'3" x 1'4.5"	56	15	8"
Company H	200 yds.	2' x 2'	90	25	9-1/2"
Company I	180 yds.	27" x 38"	105	68	8-13/16"
Company K	180 yds.	4' square	73	58	9"

Regulation uniform coat, trousers, and forage cap for the U.S.S.S. The garments shown — now in the National Museum of American History — were the official patterns, bearing red wax seals indicating approval by the Quartermaster General of the Army. They are of green woolen, the coat being of a very dark hue, the trousers and cap somewhat lighter in shade. The buttons, which were intended to be non-reflective, appear to be made of hard rubber. The coat buttons bear an eagle with the letter "I" inside the recessed shield at the center. The cap buttons are plain. (photo by Laurie Minor, Smithsonian Inst.)

Although by that time the men had learned the performance of their rifles well, it had been apparent from the beginning that practice target shooting was far different from marksmanship under combat conditions. "Shooting skill may fail even a champion marksman in battle when bullets pass right over or next to [one's] head, ...[and] when calculation of distance is out of the question because positions are changed from minute to minute," observed an experienced sharpshooter.[62]

With the approach of spring in 1862, the men anticipated active service and began their final preparations, withstanding the absence of their promised breechloading rifles. Yet regiment after regiment marched off into Virginia while the sharpshooters remained in camp. "I think we will never leave this ground until we start for home," wrote a disillusioned private. "I shall feel chagrined if I have to go back without having a chance to test my courage in battle...." Problems with obtaining their weapons had contributed to the delay in their departure. Finally, on March 20th the 1st and 2d U.S.S.S. broke camp and marched over the Long Bridge into Virginia. The feelings of the men, said an officer, "was a mixture of joy and sadness, hopes and fears," which followed from the long pent up anxiety of first facing the enemy.[63]

As to be expected, the sharpshooters' inexperience in combat was quickly evident once in the field. Reluctantly both sharpshooter regiments had accepted Colt 5 shot revolving rifle muskets until their belatedly ordered Sharps arrived. When a "scout" detachment from the 1st regiment was detailed to guard the front of their division against surprise one night in April, the detachment of scouts, expecting to be relieved momentarily, emptied their Colt rifles by firing off the chambers. The relief detachment, however, had become turned around in the darkness and approached the post from the direction of the enemy. Having unloaded guns, the original guard detail scrambled to the rear in confusion, loading their Colts as rapidly as possible. Halting a short distance away they raised their rifles and prepared to fire at the oncoming squad. At the last minute, a warning shout saved a disastrous mistake, and it was then realized the approaching soldiers were their relief. Another similar incident resulted in the death of Brigadier General C.C. Augur's orderly, who was killed by his own sharpshooter pickets when he attempted to deliver orders to a detachment of the 2d U.S. Sharpshooters

Horace Kimble, 1st N.Y. Battalion of Sharpshooters, with his telescopic target rifle, photographed in New York. (Michael J. McAfee Coll.)

just before daylight.

Also there were examples of the sharpshooters' rather casual and often unbridled attitude. While camped near the enemy Private William Straw of Company C, 1st Sharpshooters, noticed a squirrel in a distant tree top and brought him down with a single shot from his globe sighted target rifle. Arrested and brought in front of Brigadier General A. J. Smith for firing within the encampment, Straw escaped punishment only when he demonstrated that he had shot the squirrel clean through the head.[64]

Once in combat, where the danger of the battlefield was an ever present factor, there was a sobering change in perspectives. Quickly apparent was the fact that expert marksmanship did not necessarily guarantee one's survival. Advancing in the forefront of McClellan's Army during the Peninsular Campaign in early April, 1862, the 1st U.S. Sharpshooters were among the first units to engage the enemy. At Yorktown, April 5th, Private John S. M. Ide of Company E, firing from the corner of an old out house with a telescopic target rifle dueled with a Confederate sharpshooter at long range. "Several shots were exchanged between these men," said an officer, and it began to take the form of a personal affair which was watched with the keenest interest...." Ide had fired again and missed, and after reloading was raising his rifle to fire once more when he was struck in the middle of the forehead and instantly killed by a shot from his antagonist.[65]

It was a lesson well learned by the sharpshooters. The enemy had some very skilled rifle shots, and unnecessary exposure even at long range was always dangerous.

Inevitably, the superior skill of Berdan's men as marksmen began to show on the battlefield. During the siege phase of the Peninsular Campaign the Berdan Sharpshooters were annoyed by an unusual opponent, a black rifleman who was quite skilled in long range marksmanship. Awaiting a favorable chance to stalk him, a sharpshooter crept forward at night and laid in wait until morning. Discovering the black firing from the second story chimney of a gutted house, Sergeant William G. Andrews of Company E drew a bead with his telescopic rifle and brought him down, much to the satisfaction of the sharpshooters.

Another expert rifle shot with his 32 pound telescopic target rifle was Private George H. Chase of Company E, 1st Sharpshooters. Better known to the men as "Old Seth," a cantankerous sort but an ardent fighter, Chase was able to crawl well in advance of the skirmish line on May 2d and virtually isolate an enemy field gun. When the enemy gunners attempted to load the piece, Chase would drive them to cover. For two days Chase was able to keep the cannon out of service remembered a fellow sharpshooter.[66]

Because most of the men were armed with the unpredictable Colt revolving rifle muskets, the opportunity for long range marksmanship was quite limited. Berdan, however, seemed to promote the general, if temporary acceptance of the Colts. When cruising down the Potomac en route to the Peninsula a private of Company G had tried their accuracy, firing 5 shots at a buoy that was allegedly 400 yards distant. Berdan, who was watching with field glasses, said two shots hit the buoy and he was satisfied. Also, there were some examples of good combat shots with the Colts. The 2d regiment had fired on a man in civilian dress lurking ahead of their skirmish line in mid March and quickly brought him down. The man was soon found to have been struck in the leg from a considerable distance by a ball from a sharpshooter's Colt rifle. Unfortunately, the man proved to be a Federal Army scout dressed in the garb of a Virginia farmer, as revealed from a pass removed from inside the frame of the man's revolver.[67]

The Colts did prove of considerable value when a skirmish line was able to gain close proximity to an emplaced Confederate field gun on April 30th. The lieutenant in charge had his men fire repeatedly at the sand bags surrounding the muzzle of the gun once it was loaded in order to foul the bore and explode the gun. On the thirteenth round the gun exploded, and the highly pleased sharpshooters took the credit.

If the Colt revolving rifles were not highly prized for their performance by the sharpshooters, their capture by the enemy was a matter of some significance. One of Company G's Colt revolving rifles had been lost on May 1st when a sharpshooter "scout," Joseph Durkee, was killed between the lines. The Confederates had gotten to the body first and had carried off his rifle and equipments, leaving behind a note saying that the rifle was in the possession of the 5th North Carolina, and they were determined to have all the Colts before long. During the later fighting on the Peninsula the 5th Wisconsin attacked the 5th North Carolina in a vicious bayonet attack and recovered the rifle for the sharpshooters.[68]

By mid May for the 1st regiment, and mid June for the 2d, the disliked Colts had been replaced by the long anticipated Sharps, and a new standard in marksmanship and effectiveness was attained.

Enabled to lie prone on the ground and reload without difficult maneuvering or personal exposure, the sharpshooters found they could fire

41

about ten shots per minute with their breechloading Sharps. Major Caspar Trepp and two companies (A and I) of the 1st S.S. engaged in a deadly duel with a Confederate battery at Garnett's Farm on June 27th, and until their ammunition ran out (a familiar complaint with breechloaders due to their greater rate of fire), the sharpshooters were able to silence the enemy's guns. At Malvern Hill on July 1st even the sharpshooters were impressed by the awesome destructive capability of their new rifles. A battery of gray horse artillery, the elite Richmond Howitzers (McCarthy's Battery), galloped into the open field within range of four companies of Berdan's sharpshooters and attempted to unlimber. Such a fusillade of bullets greeted the artillerists that they were unable to fire a single shot before the survivors sought shelter in a nearby woods. After the war a survivor told a sharpshooter officer: "We went in a battery and came out a wreck. We staid ten minutes by the watch and came out with one gun, ten men and two horses, and without firing a shot." Special commendation had been given to the sharpshooters during the Peninsular Campaign by various generals, but the burgeoning confidence of the men, now specially equipped and battle tested, was far more meaningful in terms of their future effectiveness.[69]

In little more than three months' service Berdan's sharpshooters had justified their crack reputation, yet they had paid a considerable price. At Glendale and Malvern Hill the 1st Sharpshooters had lost two of their best officers.

Captain Edward Drew of the Wisconsin company (G) was firing a Sharps in the ranks, desperately attempting to aid in holding off the charging Confederates at Glendale June 30th 1862 when one of his sergeants was killed. Drew, on his knees, was pushing another round into his Sharps when struck in the head by a rifle ball and instantly killed.

Two days later at Malvern Hill the popular Lieutenant Colonel William Y. W. Ripley was wounded in the right leg by a musket ball, which shattered the bone. His orderly tied a handkerchief around the leg and Ripley stayed in the saddle. Finally fainting from a loss of blood, he fell from his horse, and was ultimately carried by stretcher to the rear. Amputation of the leg was narrowly averted, and due to the disabling wound Ripley never was able to return to field command, soon vacating

Sgt. James W. Staples, Co. G, 1st U.S. Sharpshooters, killed in action, Glendale, Va., June 30, 1862. (from C.A. Stevens; **Berdan's U.S. Sharpshooters in the Army of the Potomac**)

his position to Caspar Trepp.[70]

Overall losses were so severe for Berdan's men during the Peninsular fighting that when President Lincoln reviewed the decimated sharpshooter ranks by moonlight in early July he allegedly told an aide: "It's too bad! But they are good what is left of them." Company G reported at the time no commissioned officers on duty and only 26 men present, with 30 men absent. Contributing to the severe decimation of the sharpshooter ranks had been sickness, disability, and a flurry of resignations among the officers. One private even died from a reaction to a vaccination, his arm being swollen grotesquely. "More men died or were discharged from sickness than were lost in battle," sadly wrote the sharpshooters' historian. It was a thus a matter of necessity that sharpshooter recruiting detachments were sent north to obtain more men. War already had become a sobering and often debilitating experience for Berdan's sharpshooters. Who would have thought, said a sharpshooter reflecting on his earlier departure into the army, that only very few of those who had waived goodby to their loved ones would return safely. "Nobody had even an inkling of the dangers and hardships that were in store for us."[71]

But the severe losses only continued. Despite the recruits added to both regiments, strengths continued to dwindle. On January 28, 1861, at the beginning of the sharpshooters' active campaigning regimental strengths had been:

	Present	Absent
1st U.S. Sharpshooters	745	75
2d U.S. Sharpshooters	720	132
total	1465	203

Combined total present and absent — 1668

On March 21, 1863 the numbers reported for both regiments were:

1st U.S. Sharpshooters	426	
2d U.S. Sharpshooters	297	
total	723	274

Combined total present and absent — 1056
[including 14 staff and 45 line officers not added to those present for both regiments total.]

Fluctuation in the 1st Sharpshooters' strength during two months in the winter of 1862 reveals how devastating active campaigning (Fredricksburg) and seasonal hardships and illnesses were to even veteran troops.[72]

1st U.S. Sharpshooters	enlisted men present
November 1, 1862	520
December 19, 1862	493
December 31, 1862	300

With regimental strengths reduced to less than half of the original totals it was of little surprise when Lt. Col. Caspar Trepp proposed a consolidation of the two sharpshooter units in March, 1863. Yet Generals Whipple and Sickles both disapproved the request, preferring to keep the regimental identities intact, and to attempt to recruit both units up to strength.[73]

Of further complication was the permanent transfer of Company L, 1st Sharpshooters to the 1st Minnesota Infantry about June 1, 1862 (including loss to Berdan of the company's Sharps rifles). Both Berdan and the captain of the company were upset about the political maneuvering that cost the sharpshooters about 100 men of their overall strength.[74]

The further practice of splitting up the sharpshooters into various small segments, to act independently under the control of different brigades and or divisions, came under close scrutiny by the men. Intended to be skirmishers and serve as advanced troops in order to impede an enemy build up and buffer the front line against attack, the sharpshooters often found themselves deployed in two to four company strength across a broad front. Because this work was so dangerous and almost continuous from day to day, losses were a daily occurrence. Only a skirmish, as reported in the newspapers, often had a special connotation to Berdan's men. "In almost all of our minor engagements somebody was killed, and, usually we lost heavier, comparatively speaking, in these affairs, than in general engagements," remembered a sharpshooter after the war. Yet in the beginning, with many commanders unfamiliar with the concept of sharpshooters, attempts were made to utilize the men as regular infantry. Caspar Trepp was so exasperated with the utilization of his detachment as ordinary troops in Martendale's Brigade in May, 1862 he offered his resignation. Even as late as the spring of 1864, when assigned to the brigade of Brigadier General Alexander Hays, the sharpshooters were accused of being "pets, and not particularly expert with the rifle."[75]

Berdan's Sharpshooters were not to be unfairly denied in their special abilities, however. It was early observed that the fighting qualities of these sharpshooters made them of unique value as skirmishers, and that, along with sniping, remained their primary role throughout the war.

"We fought pretty much on our own hook," was the way a 1st U.S. Sharpshooter corporal described the fight at Gaines' Mill, which was typical of many sharpshooter actions. The oncoming enemy was encountered at about 50 yards, said the man, who fired his Sharps as fast as the cartridges could be inserted, the distance being so short that careful aim was unnecessary. Yet a line of skirmishers, no matter how well armed, was seldom able to hold back regimental or brigade strength battle lines of enemy troops, and the sharpshooters learned to be proficient at running. At Malvern Hill Corporal William C. Kent of Company F found the pressure too great from an attacking gray line, and responding to the bugle call to retreat, turned his back on the enemy "only while we loaded." Facing about and firing, then running away and loading, Kent soon found his Sharps too hot to hold. Yet he remained "perfectly cool." After pausing a short while for his rifle to cool, Kent continued to shoot at the enemy "as well as I know how," despite "a most ardent desire to try my legs."[76]

The furious fighting spirit of many of the men further added to the sharpshooters' rugged reputation. At Second Bull Run Private Robert Casey of Company G, 1st S.S., was struck in the throat. Suddenly jumping to his feet, wild with shock and excitement, Casey furiously gestured with his rifle and began swearing mightily until the blood gurgled in his throat and prevented speech. He then fired his remaining cartridges fully exposed and with reckless abandon. When down to his last round, no enemy being in view, he shot at a hog running through the brush, then slowly walked from the field indifferent to the bullets and shell whistling about him.[77]

The prevalence of many such characters in both regiments had contributed to the notoriety of the Berdan Sharpshooters, both for their reckless effectiveness in combat and sheer cussedness in camp. Among the legendary characters of the 1st regiment was Private Truman Head of Company C, better known as "California Joe." Of all the quasi celebrities in camp during the winter of 1861-1862, "Old Californ'y," as he was sometimes called, was perhaps the best known. At age 52 he had come East from California to enlist in the war effort, perhaps intending to join Edward D. Baker's 71st Pennsylvania, which was known as the "California Regiment." The allure of special service as a scout and sharpshooter was evidently more appealing, for in September, 1861 he enlisted with Berdan and was assigned to Company C. Joe's background of grizzly bear hunting and the Gold Rush made him a great

One of the most famous of sharpshooter photographs. Colonel Hiram Berdan and "California Joe,"
Private Truman Head, Co. C, 1st U.S.S.S. Photographed in early Sept. 1862 in the vicinity of
Washington, D.C. Recently recovered from illness during the Peninsular campaign, Joe was back in the
hospital with jaundice on Sept. 12th. Col. Berdan, who remained on sick leave until Dec. 17th, shows
little sign of the "wound" suffered a few days earlier at the Second Bull Run. (Courtesy Vermont
Historical Society)

favorite with the men. Described as past fifty, but looking "a score of
years younger," he was said to stand "straight as an arrow," with "an eye
as keen as a hawk, nerves as steady as can be, and an endowment of hair
and whiskers Reubens would have liked for a patriarchal portrait."

Almost a father figure to many of the men, Joe had quickly earned
their respect when during a sudden confused fire fight at Munson's Hill
on September 29, 1861 he had prevented a serious mistake. It was at
night and the rain was falling when an officer rode up and ordered a
charge against troops then firing toward them from a nearby woods.
"Old Californ'y" stepped from the ranks and accosted the officer: "You

damned fool, do you want to charge our own men?" After some heated verbal bantering Joe went down toward the woods and brought back a Union soldier. When asked how he had known in the darkness they were Federals, Joe replied that when their guns flashed he could see the profile of their caps, and knew they were not enemy troops.

Joe's exploits and background had been widely publicized by the press, and he was the first man in the regiment to be armed with a Sharps rifle, buying his own by private purchase while in Camp of Instruction at Washington, D.C. Joe's expertise and experience, in fact, may have had a significant bearing on the decision of Berdan's men to adopt the Sharps rifle over all other competing weapons.

Once in active combat on the Peninsula, Joe's reputation only intensified. During a lull in one fight Joe showed up in the camp of the 5th New York Infantry (Duryea's Zouaves) seeking ammunition for his then singular Sharps rifle. A captain quickly furnished him with a liberal supply, two companies of the 5th being armed with the Sharps. Joe, who had been at the front all day "picking off the enemy's gunners," then hastened back to the battle line after thanking the captain, saying "he wouldn't waste them, you bet." On another occasion Joe had been in camp one night with some men of Company G, when a stranger came in and lay down by him. From his casual conversation it was soon heard that the man was from a Louisiana battalion. Instantly, California Joe and another man sprang on top of the startled man, choking him to "within an inch of his life." One observer later reflected how unfortunate it was for the obviously lost Rebel to have chosen that particular spot to have crawled into.

California Joe's marksmanship in combat and his legendary exploits soon earned him widespread national fame. Despite contrived and inaccurately inflated accounts in Northern newspapers which added to Joe's wild and ferocious reputation, California Joe actually was short in stature (5'7") and a mild mannered man — "the gentlest of men," said the sharpshooters' historian. He was "entirely free from brag and bluster, [and] an unassuming man," he added. Indeed, Old Californ'y was both friendly and a "hero in spite of himself." When during the night of April 11, 1862 Joe was reportedly shot, the sharpshooters' camp was said to be "wild" with anxiety over the rapidly spreading rumor. Actually, it turned out that Joe in a skirmish between picket squads had taken a rifle ball on the barrel band of his Sharps, snapping it off and driving it against Joe's nose and cheek. This had caused profuse bleeding but only

A posed photograph of "California Joe Watching for Rebs." Another of the early Sept. 1862 photographs taken while Joe was recovering at Washington, D.C. from disability. (Courtesy Vermont Historical Society)

a superficial wound.

Yet Joe's days with the sharpshooters were numbered. His age had conspired against him, and following Malvern Hill Joe's eyes were so debilitated by the sun's glare and dust that he was admitted to a Washington hospital. After briefly rejoining his regiment in early September, during which time he posed for several photographs with Colonel Berdan, Joe re-entered the hospital on September 12, 1862 with jaundice. Within a few months he was discharged for disability and soon returned to California, living at San Francisco where he became a customs inspector. Until his death November 24, 1874, he no longer was Truman Head, but "California Joe," and allegedly signed all but his legal documents with that cherished nom de guerre.[78]

If "California Joe" seemed to reflect a unique aspect of the sharpshooters, there were many other characters sprinkled throughout their ranks that had earned a notoriety of sorts. "Swearing Bob" was Robert Casey of the 1st regiment, so named for the epithets he invariably hurled at the enemy in combat. "Shoot and swear, swear and shoot," was his method said an officer, especially after he was nicked in the finger at Glendale. Another member of Company G, "Snap Shot," was found to be wearing a patented vest of armor in the fight at Hanover on May 27th, 1862. "Old Seth" of the New Hampshire company (E), George H. Chase, was a dedicated killer who carried an enormous target rifle, being known as a rambunctious sort who never enjoyed laying around camp. Another man, "Buckshot," was on the heavy side and was given the prominent center spot in his company. A sharpshooter favorite, "Tommy," Thomas McCaul of Company G, had gone into the fight at Gaines' Mill wearing a conspicuous straw hat. When the enemy's fire began to be concentrated on his location, McCaul cast the hat out from behind the stump where he was hiding, causing laughter heard over the sound of fighting, said an onlooker.[79]

That Berdan's sharpshooters were able to retain a spirit of levity amid the trauma of intense fighting was in essence a measure of their inner fiber and organizational merit. No matter how severe the disaster or adverse the conditions the men always seemed to share a joke or carry on in a carefree manner. The sharpshooters functioned much as team, with pride and confidence in their abilities, yet with a discerning and fundamental knowledge that although certain matters were beyond their control life would be much as what they made of it. The "boys" were always looking for some fun to "lighten the load," even in their most difficult circumstances. When a sharpshooter returned from leave in Wisconsin with a bottle of wine and a box of Fox Lake cigars, his entire company seemed to have marched off to battle at Mechanicsville smoking cigars and with a smile on their face.

During their first night on the Peninsula the sharpshooters had held an impromptu beach party at Hampton Roads, wading waist deep into the ocean to gather oysters, clams, and muscles. Amid the blazing campfires the odor of roasting shellfish and hearty laughter wafted on the breeze. Following a feast of roast clams, fried oysters, stewed periwinkles, and boiled muscles, there was a rousing concert of spontaneous songs, including "John Brown's Body," and even "Dixie," evidently for the benefit of the nearby Rebel pickets.[80]

Ever a passion among the sharpshooters, as well as many other units, was the favorite pastime of gambling. When ever time permitted a game of cards seemed to be in progress, often with a more than nominal amount of money at stake. "Enemy" chickens and geese seemed to be everywhere encountered along the march, and even Lieutenant Colonel Francis Peteler of the 2d regiment managed to "capture" a half dozen geese with his revolver while near the Chancellor House in July, 1862. Another favorite chicken story of the sharpshooters involved Colonel Berdan, who heard a live chicken "peeping" from inside a haversack in Company A while on a long march. Orders having been published against foraging, and with the chicken continually sounding out, Berdan could not well pretend he didn't hear it, said an officer. Berdan had the man arrested and placed under guard at the rear of the regiment. When questioned by the colonel the next day why he was under arrest, the man replied, "for stealing a chicken." Berdan sent him back to the guards. Several days later the same scene was repeated. Finally, on the third attempt, when asked why he was under arrest, the man replied: "For not having cut the chicken's head off." Berdan promptly restored him to duty. "There were no more chickens carried alive in the haversacks," wryly recorded the sharpshooters' historian.

The fun loving Swiss of Company A were fond of teasing a recent immigrant from Zurich who spoke broken English. When he referred in camp to a bird that cries "cuckoo" as a nightingale, the men well remembered his mistake. When on a march, someone in the ranks would invariably call out, "What does the nightingale say?" Immediately, a dozen men would burst out — "cuckoo, cuckoo!" — to the laughter of the entire company.[81]

Being well adapted veterans after their first campaign the sharpshooters were familiar with the Army routine, and did not hesitate to break rules or regulations if to their advantage. Evidently arranging a truce with their Confederate counterparts while on picket at Sulphur Springs, Va. in August, 1863, the sharpshooters were found swimming, washing their laundry, and lounging at their posts by their strict brigade commander. The incident nearly resulted in a court martial of the sharpshooters' commander by the thoroughly angry general.[82]

If their attitude sometimes seemed to others to be overly casual or jaunty, it masked only the supreme terror of individual trauma, the uncertainty of one's personal fate and survival amid one of the most difficult combat roles in the entire Army. The experience of Private James

Winchell of Company D, 1st S.S. at Gaines' Mill provides a graphic example of what was in store for many sharpshooter victims of war's terrible fury.

Winchell was struck in the left arm by a rifle ball during a reconnaissance on June 27th. He then painfully made his way to a small brick house about 500 yards distant where he fell into the enemy's hands about an hour later. Here Winchell noted that his wound was particularly ugly, the ball having struck about midway between the elbow and shoulder and shattered the bone as it passed through. The brick house was being used as a hospital and although the battle raged about them, the surgeons remained at work throughout. Winchell had no place to prop his head up as he lay on the floor while musket balls and even a stray shell ripped through the windows and tore into the walls. Finally an attendant provided a severed leg for a pillow, much to Winchell's distress. When the doctor hurriedly looked at him, he poked his thumb through the open wound, bandaged it, and merely said the arm would have to be amputated.

The following morning Winchell was carried outside and placed on the ground in the hot sunshine while Confederate officers made their rounds. There were so many wounded from both armies that each wounded Federal had to wait his turn, according to the preference of the Confederate surgeons. Winchell painfully crawled into the shade of a small scrub oak where he remained for day after day. With only some straw and several barrel staves for a pillow, Winchell endured the intense heat and swarms of fleas, mosquitoes, flies, and maggots. The flies were the worst, said Winchell, and his right arm ached constantly, so tired was he in attempting to keep them away. When ever he asked for treatment he was always told: "yes, as soon as we get through with a few bad cases."

By the fourth day, with his wound still festering, Winchell had all but given up hope. There was nothing to eat but a few bites of stale biscuit and occasionally some black raspberries.

Finally, about noon on the fourth day a Dr. White, said to be a captured surgeon from Massachusetts who was still attending the wounded, came to Winchell and told him: "Young man are you going to have your arm taken off, or are you going to lie here and let the maggots eat you up?" When asked if Dr. White had any chloroform or whiskey to ease the pain, White replied: "no, and I have no time to dilly dally with you." Winchell reluctantly agreed, and was led to the amputation table. After cutting off his shirt, filled with maggots, and poking fingers through the wound, which seemed particularly cruel, they made him sit up in a chair. Then, in Winchell's own words: "[they] wanted to hold my legs, but I said 'no, I won't kick you, but steady my shoulders.' [I] then set my teeth together and clinched my [right] hand into my hair, and told them to go on. After cutting the top part of my arm and taking out the bone, they wanted me to rest ... I refused, as they had mangled my arm I wanted but one job of it, for I was just as ready... to kick the bucket then as in another hour. ...Then they finished it, while I gasped for breath and the lower jaw dropped in spite of my firm clinch. I was then led away a short distance and left to lie on the hot sand — like a bake oven — and could feel the hairs crawl on my head as large apparently as my fingers. Burning with fiery pain, flushed with the fiery hot bed of sand, I arose wild with the pain and extreme heat, and began to look for a cooler place to lie down to die...."

In his delirium Winchell stumbled up the stairs of the brick house, now a hospital, and crawled next to a man lying on a bed. "If I had just entered into a furnace I would not have burned with more pain and fever," said Winchell. Unable to stand the agony, he bolted down the stairs to his oak tree in the shade, where he "rolled and groaned with burning pains until a captain of the 14th [U.S.] Regulars told me to ...lie down and keep still, that the rolling only made me feel worse." Finally heeding his advice, Winchell was better able to endure the pain, and considered that this timely advice probably saved his life.

For the next twelve days Winchell remained under the scrub oak, enduring three days and nights of rain with only a few sips of brandy to help him through. Later transported by Army wagon to Savage Station (a ride taken at a fast trot to the sheer agony of the amputees), then by freight train to Richmond, Winchell was finally exchanged in July at City Point, Va. After being sent to Pennsylvania for a long stay at West Philadelphia Hospital (subject to the often harsh treatment of medical students), Winchell was finally discharged September 18, 1862.[83]

Such trauma truly defies description. Yet it was the lot of thousands of soldiers on both sides, many of whom failed to survive the medical ignorance and abominable sanitary conditions that were so prevalent. If the sharpshooters' growing resentment of those who failed to share such dangers was evident in their actions, such as their disgust when inspected and found "exceedingly unmilitary" by a staff officer in winter camp during 1862, their derision was fully justified in the eyes of many of their fellow soldiers. This inspection, in fact, delineated the enormous difference in the administration of a fighting unit by combat officers, as opposed to the "regulations" mentality in which appearance and camp discipline dominated in an evaluation.

In contrast to the findings of staff officer Lieutenant Colonel Bartram, who wrote that they were "slouches and slovens" in appearance and deficient as a military organization, the sharpshooters were regarded by Lieutenant Colonel Caspar Trepp to be combat ready and of good discipline and appearance in the same inspection report filed a few weeks earlier.

As the sharpshooters well knew, fighting ability and effectiveness was not adequately measured by uniformity of dress and presence of extraneous equipment. Bartram observed that "hardly any two [men] are uniformed alike, and about half the men are without bayonets." He seemed almost incredulous when noting that this seemed to be as a result of the dictates of the men themselves. [84]

After more than a year of active service, it was evident that the men cared less about how they looked than how well they lived and fought. Following a few months in the field a recruit wrote home to his wife, "you would not know us. We are black and dirty." If bedraggled, and found wearing a mixture of blue fatigue jackets, green coats, and light blue pants, the bronzed faces, faded clothes, and tattered banners told all too well of their arduous service. Due to Berdan's insistence, however, following the disastrous inspection in December, 1862 a new issue of green uniforms was promptly forthcoming (issued on January 5th). On January 12, 1863 a private of Company I wrote, "The men look nice all dressed in green and their brass plates shining. This is the best dressed regiment I have seen. The other soldiers here say they wish they had such clothes and such guns." [85]

Even more significant was the matter of the missing angular bayonets. Originally issued with their Sharps rifles, by the end of the Peninsular Campaign much of the 1st regiment had been given permission to discard them as unnecessary and cumbersome. This entire matter came into sharp focus during Berdan's court martial, and further reflected the

---

The face of a veteran and the d.s.t. Sharps rifle of a sharpshooter. The best of the Union Army in 1862. (Herb Peck, Jr. collection)

unwillingness of these special duty troops to carry unnecessary equipment into combat. Despite the sharpshooters' complaints, by mid 1863 they were required to carry bayonets again; "our regiment has all had to take new bayonets; that makes the boys mad again, you know," said a member of Company K, 1st Sharpshooters.[86]

Difficulty with the army bureaucracy had already taken its toll in morale following the issue of shoddy clothing, short rations, the absence of pay for six months, and the loss of their knapsacks on the Peninsula — which when returned several months later had been plundered. By the onset of their second year's campaigning the veterans of Berdan Sharpshooters were "Army wise" and unwilling to endure petty treatment or even the brazen threats of generals. When Brigadier General John H. (Hobart) Ward, their brigade commander, threatened to shoot Bill Sweet of Company G on the spot for some trivial offense there was an immediate confrontation. "He was going to blow hard-tack through (Bill Sweet's) heart," said a sharpshooter, "when every rifle hammer in the company [G] cocked. He heard the click-click, and lowering his revolver, rode off swearing hard at us." Indeed, the sharpshooters' no-nonsense reputation often earned them a considerable amount of respect. They performed but little fatigue duty, and were often given preferential treatment when in camp. Their popularity with the other units of the Army, however, often suffered. Captain John B. Isler of Company A reported how the sharpshooters seemed to be "hated by all that have to deal with [us]."[87]

Toughened and prepared for the arduous service which they knew was in store for them, the Berdan Sharpshooters had marched off to fight at such battles as Second Bull Run, Antietam, and Chancellorsville with their eyes open and their familiar Sharps at the ready.

Second Bull Run was particularly devastating for the 1st U.S.S.S., the regiment sustaining a loss of 65 out of 290 present while fighting against Stonewall Jackson's troops. The 2d Sharpshooters reportedly expended 200,000 rounds of ammunition during Pope's Campaign, and saw their strength dwindle from more than 600 on August 11th to 127 men on September 2d.

At Antietam the 1st Sharpshooters remained in reserve but the 2d regiment was in the thickest of action at the cornfield and "Bloody Lane," losing 66 men, about one fourth of their strength. The 2d Sharpshooters and their Sharps rifles were particularly effective here, as their colonel wrote: "while lying on their faces on the open ground they did more damage to the enemy than any brigade in our front or to our right, we firing obliquely." When a burial detail put 192 Confederate corpses into a single grave site at this point, the 2d U.S.S.S. claimed much of the credit for these casualties.[88]

After the Army reorganization that sent the sharpshooters from the 5th Corps to the 3rd Corps during the winter of 1862-1863, both regiments served together as a single unit at Chancellorsville. It was a unique and enlightening circumstance, and resulted in the capture of 365 officers and men of the 23d Georgia at the "Cedars" on May 2d. So many Sharps rifles in one location had so devastated the Georgians that they had taken cover in a railroad cut where most were flanked and captured by 60 men of the 1st Sharpshooters on the right flank. The next day both regiments were in the hottest of the fighting in the heavy thickets along the 3rd Corps line. Yet much of the command had been broken up into the usual small detachments to serve as snipers and skirmishers. One sharpshooter detachment of about 80 men charged some of Stonewall Jackson's men and captured more prisoners before being withdrawn. In all, Chancellorsville had earned the sharpshooters high honors, one brigade commander in his official report praising them "as one of the best organizations in the volunteer service."[89]

Despite the prominence given to their reconnaissance to Pitzer's Woods, the sharpshooters' greatest contribution at Gettysburg was their effort during the furious fighting with Longstreet's men in the Emmitsburg Road and Little Round Top sectors. A consideration not often mentioned by historians is the devastating effect their breechloaders had in helping throw back attack after attack against these critical positions. The 2d U.S.S.S. was heavily engaged in the Little Round Top fight and Colonel William C. Oates of the 15th Alabama regiment paid high tribute to the work of the 2d Sharpshooters in a lengthy post war letter to Lieutenant Colonel H.R. Stoughton. Noting his loss of 23 officers and 423 men from a total strength of 42 officers and 644 men, Oates said "you and your command deserve a monument for turning the tide in favor of the Union cause." Oates specifically mentioned the untenable position he was placed in when within 120 yards of Little Round Top. "A moment later you appeared directly in my rear and opened fire on me. I then occupied the ledge of rocks from which I had driven the 20th Maine. That and a New York regiment [44th, and also the 83d Pennsylvania] assailing me in front and you in the rear, forced my thinned ranks to face and fire in both directions, which we could not long endure."[Actually, only a portion of the 2d Sharpshooters was present in any one spot along the Little Round Top line during the crisis, but among the most important were about 15 or 20 sharpshooters who fought alongside Company B of the 20th Maine on the extreme left flank.][90]

To the sharpshooters' battle wise veterans of Gettysburg and other hard fought actions the affair at Wapping Heights, July 23, 1863 must have seemed like a welcome respite. The 1st Sharpshooters were on the skirmish line, advancing in the brush against a slowly withdrawing enemy line when they encountered blackberries in "endless quantities." The boys wrote an observer, were picking and shooting until their supply of 60 rounds was gone, then slinging their rifles over their shoulders "they went for the blackberries with both hands." One overly eager picker, Lute Harrington of Company F, suddenly found himself face to face with two Confederates, one of whom had just fired, and the other was in the act of loading his muzzle loader. Swinging his empty breechloader from his shoulder, he covered the two Confederates and marched them to the rear, they not discovering the Sharps was empty until safely in the hands of the provost. One amazed foreign officer who was observing the whole scene was heard to exclaim, "Mine Got! vat kind of men have got up dere to pick blackberries on der skirmish line?"[91]

The Berdan Sharpshooters were no ordinary troops, as they had well demonstrated on many fields. They were versatile, as at Auburn, Va. October 13, 1863, when the sharpshooters fixed their seldom used angular bayonets and led a successful charge over open ground into a woods. They were durable, as in the aftermath of Chancellorsville, where the men were on picket for 17 hours without eating or sleeping. Most of all they were reliable, and when in combat there were few units that could match their fighting prowess. Their own major seemed to touch upon the real basis for the efficacy of the sharpshooters when he wrote of his puzzlement at the sharpshooters' success at Chancellorsville. "The complete and almost instant success of a mere line of skirmishers in turning back the enemy approaching in force ...I confess, surprised me. How much of that success is to be attributed to the superior skill of these skirmishers as marksmen, how much to the rapidity with which their

A youthful sharpshooter with his d.s.t. Sharps and angular bayonet, ca. 1863. (Herb Peck, Jr. collection)

Sharps rifles can be loaded and fired, [and] how much to the remarkable coolness and steadiness of the men themselves, ...I do not pretend to judge."[92]

Despite their importance and success, with the onset of the 1864 campaign the sharpshooters' days were numbered. During January, 1864 the government offered a bounty of $400 and a thirty day furlough to two year veterans who would re-enlist. To men such as William B. Greene of Company G, 2d S.S. who had been made many promises but had only been paid a cumulative total of $55.81 up to December, 1863, the government's incentives may not have been so alluring. Only a few of the 1st Sharpshooters accepted the offer, said their historian. In the 2d regiment most of the veterans apparently re-enlisted, but their numbers were too few to sustain the organization indefinitely (the 2d regiment had only eight companies, while the 1st had ten).[93]

Throughout the period of "modern warfare" combat involving entrenchments and breastworks which characterized the last year of the war in the Eastern theater, the role of the sharpshooters was prominent. From the Wilderness through the siege of Petersburg both sharpshooter regiments were in the thickest of the fighting as a part of the II Corps. At Spottsylvania the Confederate dead were found to be lying in piles outside of the sharpshooters' position in front of the captured enemy works, five separate charges being driven back at this point. "The conduct of our soldiers... was never better than in this day's fight," thought Captain Charles A. Stevens. By the Battle of Cold Harbor in early June, 1864 the sharpshooters had been under fire twenty-four out of thirty-one days during the campaign. It was a dubious distinction that would continue. The sharpshooters' role as skirmishers was of primary importance in the flanking movements that characterized Grant's campaigning from the Rapidan to the James. The 1st Sharpshooters numbered only 175 men present with a captain commanding when they fought at Harrison's Creek on June 16, 1864. During the Petersburg fighting they continued to lose heavily, including several officers who had been with the regiment from the beginning of their service. Lieutenant Colonel Stoughton of the 2d regiment who had been wounded May 9th in fighting along the Po River, returned to duty on June 21st, only to be captured a few hours later when sent by his brigade commander against overwhelming numbers along the Jerusalem Plank Road. Men such as these could not be easily replaced, nor were they.[94]

The government's policy of assigning recruits to new regiments rather than filling up the veteran units was particularly devastating to the sharpshooters with their greater exposure and thus higher loss ratio. Company D of the 1st regiment failed to obtain a single recruit prior to their muster out during November, 1864. Beginning on August 18th with Company A, the Swiss and Germans, the 1st Sharpshooters were mustered out of the Army due to expiration of their three years' term of service. Of the 106 men present in the company in 1861 twelve remained at the muster out. In Company C there were five of the original 101. Between August and December, 1864 all but Companies I and K of the 1st U.S.S.S. were mustered out. The remaining two companies served as a consolidated battalion until December 31st, when they were transferred to the 2d regiment.[95]

By February 20, 1865 the final call to arms had sounded for the Sharpshooters. The 2d U.S.S.S. was disbanded and the men with unexpired terms of service were assigned to various state regiments. Their record had been without parallel during the war. Innovative in concept and utilizing advanced technology, they were in a certain measure the predecessors of special forces units — the green berets. Not only had the Sharpshooters killed more individual enemy soldiers than any other comparably sized unit, but they had established a new standard in fighting efficacy. "We are justly proud of [our record]," wrote a sharpshooter after the war. "No other regiment in the army surpassed us."[96]

Indeed, perhaps the greatest tribute to the Berdan Sharpshooters came from their opponents, the men who had to face those deadly Sharps rifles; "the Sharpshooters were the worst men we have to contend with," said a Confederate officer after the Gettysburg fight. The notoriety of Berdan's men as deadly killers had in large part accounted for the attitude of many in both armies that sharpshooters were little better than wanton murderers. Captive Confederate sharpshooters taken in the Devil's Den at Gettysburg had expected to be hung as snipers, said one of Berdan's amused officers, noting that they did not realize that they had been captured by Berdan's Sharpshooters.[97]

Proud and unsubdued, the skeleton remnant of these original sharpshooters had turned their faces homeward with only a few months left in the war. "At last all was over," wrote a field officer, noting his men's reluctance to turn in their trusty Sharps rifles, "to which they had become attached by long companionship in many scenes of danger and death."

Years later when the returning veterans dedicated a monument at Gettysburg, depicted on the granite face were crossed target and Sharps rifles above a swarming nest of hornets. As the dedication speaker proudly noted, the hornets' nest had derived from the name given to the sharpshooters by some of their captives from Hood's division at Gettysburg after facing their deadly Sharps on Little Round Top, July 2, 1863. Said a sharpshooter in reflection: what greater distinction can anyone boast than having been a sharpshooter. Today, it seems that in many ways Berdan's Sharpshooters had, indeed, been "hornets" among ordinary mortals.[98]

Sharps #56113

PART III:
THE BERDAN SHARPS RIFLES

The Sharps rifle, reported a prestigious Board of Ordnance shortly before the Civil War, "is superior to any of the other arms loading at the breech." About the same time a veteran regular officer volunteered his opinion "as to the superiority of Sharps' rifle...over all other arms for sporting and military purposes." "In all military operations where a bayonet is not required, as in scouting, skirmishing, and particularly for mounted service," he continued, "it is without an equal." Yet Hiram Berdan, the man who would do more for the reputation of the Sharps rifle than any other during the Civil War, at the beginning of his military service was unconvinced about the desirability of the Sharps for his sharpshooters.[99]

Shortly after receiving authority for the organization of the sharpshooters Berdan wrote on July 19, 1861 to the Chief of Ordnance, Brigadier General James W. Ripley:

I have tried the Springfield rifle musket and much prefer it to anything I have seen and would like 750 of them for my regiment. Can't you manage to give me this number? You can't place them where they will do equal service, and I will regard it as a special favor.

Ripley later reported that he placed Springfield rifle muskets at the Washington Arsenal for Berdan's requisition, and later Harper's Ferry rifles with sword bayonets [Model 1855 rifles], but Berdan failed to obtain them.[100]

This request, of course, proved to be a major faux pas on the part of Berdan, who soon was seeking breechloading rifles for his men. Many of his sharpshooters were recruited believing they would be armed with breechloaders equipped with telescopic sights. By early September, 1861 with the various sharpshooter companies beginning to rendezvous at Camp of Instruction in Washington, Berdan was actively attempting to fulfill these unofficial promises.[101]

The first order of business was to determine which breechloading rifle was the most suitable for his sharpshooters. For some time Berdan had been seeking sample arms of various types to try, and Sharps was among the companies solicited for an appropriate arm. Evidently Berdan had been attempting to get a sample to his specification from Sharps prior to September 21, 1861, when he telegraphed to Richard S. Lawrence of Sharps: "When will the sample rifle be here without fail. Answer immediately."[102]

Possibly this sample rifle was fitted with a heavy octagon barrel and had special globe sights. An order for a custom Sharps weighing about 20 pounds, apparently for Berdan's trial, is said to be noted in the Sharps records. An article in the Detroit Free Press of the period stated: "The guns which have just been ordered by the government [incorrectly reported] at a cost of sixty or seventy dollars each are Sharps improved target rifle[s] with globe sights, rifle stock, octagon barrel, double triggers, patch falls [patched ball, or probably patch box], etc. Colonel Berdan writes that 'this gun, taking all kinds of weather, in a thorough trial here, has beaten all the target rifles at anything over 60 rods. The new guns will be much finer sighted, of course, than the old, and will be in my judgment, a very superior gun for sharpshooters. Of course, all who have favorite guns of their own which they wish to bring are at liberty to do so.'"[103]

Interestingly, following a number of trials at the sharpshooters' camp during early and mid October, 1861, the Sharps rifle was selected. Yet it was of a relatively basic design, being a standard New Model 1859 military rifle fitted with double set triggers and equipped for the saber bayonet. On October 22, 1861 Berdan wrote to Simon Cameron, Secretary of War describing his men's preference:

The bearer has a sample gun, one of Sharps improved pattern & a new bayonet which I think may interest you. I have selected this gun as the most suitable weapon to be placed in the hands of my sharpshooters that I know of.

In fact any of the ordinary weapons would make my men little better than the common infantry & as my men are getting in very good drill no time should be lost in arming & sending them forward.

Mr. J.C. Palmer, Prest. of the Sharp[s] Mang. Compy. informs me that he can furnish say 3000 of these guns commencing to give us 100 a day after 20 days on receipt of the order & without any interference with the present Government order for carbines. We have about 200 heavy target rifles which is as many as I care to have of these heavy guns. We are exceedingly anxious to have these improved breechloaders with long bayonets. The price in $43 but this includes fly lock, double triggers & the *long bayonet with sheath. The additional charge of 50 cts. over the ordinary gun is certainly very reasonable for the extra work.*

The men as well as myself feel that with these weapons we can not only make a name for ourselves but be of vast service to the country.[104]

Considerable speculation exists that Berdan sent a sample rifle with California Joe (Pvt. Truman Head, Co. C) on the mission to see Cameron. California Joe is known to have had his own Sharps rifle, purchased privately while at Camp of Instruction near Washington. Joe's rifle, however, was a New Model 1859 fitted with a single trigger, and equipped for the saber bayonet. It was to remain the only Sharps rifle carried in the sharpshooter regiments until early May, 1862.

According to Captain C.A. Stevens, the sharpshooters had carefully examined Joe's weapon and endorsed it over the multitude of other weapons offered by various manufacturers. It thus appears that California Joe's personal weapon was much the basis for the final selection, the addition of double set triggers being the only modification utilized from the special sample weapon or weapons supplied by Sharps. Apparently the Sharps octagon barrel target rifle was considered as too heavy for ordinary field use. Also, the much greater cost for special equipment such as globe sights would be objectionable to the government. Further, California Joe's older, almost fatherly image, his prominent reputation based upon his experience hunting grizzly bears in the West, and his demonstrated skill in the action on September 29, 1861 at Munson's Hill may have been persuading factors. The men's preference for the Sharps became so great that they insisted on these arms, even when great obstacles soon were thrown in their path.[105]

Incredibly, a month after writing to Cameron about the Sharps, Berdan was endorsing a proposal to obtain for his men Colt Revolving rifle muskets. The difficulty in obtaining an order from the Ordnance Department for the desired Sharps rifles apparently had changed Berdan's approach. This resistance is believed to have involved both the Ordnance Department's objection to non standardized weapons for infantry, and their long existing and unfilled contract for cavalry carbines with the Sharps company. On June 29, 1861 the Ordnance Department had purchased 3,000 Sharps carbines on contract. Less than a week later they had ordered another 3,000. In December Brigadier General Ripley expanded the order to all the carbines Sharps could manufacture until further notice. Deliveries of these carbines was so slow, the second order for 3,000 not being completed until January 18, 1862, that the entire factory was clogged with delayed production. Sharps' production rate remained at the less than satisfactory figure of about 50 arms (carbines) per day throughout the winter of 1861-1862. Although J. C. Palmer of Sharps was said to be promising delivery of the Berdan special order rifles in less than thirty days from receipt of the order, and without disrupting the carbine contract, this was unrealistic since the Sharps production rate was limited regardless of rifle or carbine manufacture. Particularly objectionable to the Ordnance Department was the prospect that they would give up the much needed Sharps carbine deliveries for perhaps two months during a changeover to rifle manufacture.[106]

Berdan, meanwhile, was most anxious about obtaining his breechloaders. He had been talking with Colt agent Hugh Harbinson, whom Samuel Colt had sent to Washington, D.C. in order to obtain the Berdan contract for breechloaders if possible. With more salesmanship than substance, Harbinson evidently promised prompt delivery of .56 caliber Model 1855 Colt Revolving Rifle Muskets (with 37-1/2" barrels), if only Berdan would get him an order. While Berdan persisted in his attempt to push the Sharps order through, with calculating acumen, he understood that the stronger political connections of the Colt firm with key Army leaders would be of great help in the overall plan to get approval of the breechloaders for his men. Perhaps anticipating that the 2d U.S. Sharpshooters would be a logical spot for the Colts, since his 1st regiment had strongly endorsed the Sharps (a total of 2,000 rifles were desired to equip both regiments), Berdan soon was playing both ends against the middle in his battle with the Ordnance Department — and Brigadier James W. Ripley, in particular.[107]

In early November, 1861 Berdan brought a Colt revolving rifle into Camp of Instruction to test. By the 13th of that month a rumor was circulating among the 2d regiment that Berdan had ordered 1,000 of these rifles for them. "The gun he brought was a Colts Rifle, Revolver, a five shooter. It was a splendid looking gun, but I think I should not like it a[s] well as a Sharps Rifle," wrote a member of Company B, 2d Sharpshooters on that date.[108]

Berdan's political ally in this special weapons project was Colonel R. B. Marcy, chief of staff to the Army of the Potomac's commander, Major General George B. McClellan. Marcy, in fact, was a major figure and the primary correspondent on Berdan's behalf in seeking the desired breechloaders. As Berdan well knew, Marcy was a personal friend of Samuel Colt and was a primary exponent of Colt arms, having written in

"Col. H. Berdan's H'dq'rs Camp of Instruction, [located at 1st & T Sts.] Washington, D.C., United States Sharpshooters," drawn by D.P. Craig, Co. A., 2d U.S.S.S., from sketch made by him in 1891. (Collection of Division of Armed Forces History, Natl. Museum of American History)

1859: "I look upon Colt's new patent rifle as a most excellent arm for border service. ...it is the most reliable and certain weapon to fire that I have ever used, ...and if I were alone upon the prairies, and expected an attack from a body of Indians, I ...[know of no other] arm I would as soon have in my hands as this."[109] [In November, 1861 Marcy, McClellan, Ripley, and Simon Cameron were among those presented with double cased sets of Colt's new model revolvers, which was part of Samuel Colt's highly effective promotion of his arms][110]

On November 23, 1861, Marcy, acting in McClellan's name, gave Colt's Hugh Harbinson a letter to be signed by McClellan that would request the Ordnance Department to order 1,000 Colt Revolving Rifle Muskets for Berdan's men. This letter was signed by McClellan on November 26th, and Harbinson proceeded to the ordnance office to confer with Ripley.

At this point the real difficulty began. Ripley had long since gone on the record (June 11, 1861) that "a great evil" existed in "the vast variety of new inventions" proposed as government small arms, which had resulted in "many kinds and calibers of arms, ...none [of which were] as good as the United States musket." "This evil," said Ripley, "can only be stopped by positively refusing to answer any requisitions for...new and untried arms, and steadily adhering to the rule of uniformity of arms for all troops...." Ripley refused when solicited by Harbinson for the Berdan order, and said that the matter would have to be referred to the Secretary of War. Harbinson went back to Marcy with the news, and the political tug of war was immediately joined.[11]

Within the next few days McClellan, Cameron, Ripley, Berdan, and even Abraham Lincoln were involved in an increasingly bitter dispute. Secretary of War Cameron referred McClellan's request of November 26th to his assistant, who sent for Ripley. Ripley and Cameron's assistant called in McClellan, who happened to be present at the time, and they collectively agreed that Berdan would get the Springfield rifle musket. The reason for McClellan's compliance, said Berdan, was because Marcy had made all the arrangements, and McClellan knew little of what was involved in his attempt to get breechloaders. When Berdan learned of what had transpired he went directly to President Lincoln, having previously entertained the president in camp during one of his Saturday target matches. Lincoln had been favorably impressed with Berdan and his men, and now agreed to endorse the request for breechloaders.

Berdan then returned to see McClellan and related the whole story. McClellan again endorsed Berdan's request for breechloaders, and even promised to personally see the Secretary of War to straighten out the matter. Marcy was instructed to write another letter, which was forwarded to Cameron on December 2d. It read as follows:

Headquarters, Army of Potomac
Washington, December 2, 1861

To the Honorable S. Cameron
Secretary of War
Sir:

General McClellan is desirous that the First Regiment of Colonel Berdan's Sharpshooters should be armed with Colt improved patent repeating rifles which have been offered to the Government at forty-five dollars each, and which offer through Colonel Berdan's effort, is seven dollars and fifty cents less than he charges the Government. This price is very low for this arm and General McClellan would be glad to have them ordered as soon as possible.

> *Yours respectfully, your obedient servant*
> *R. B. Marcy*
> *Chief of Staff*

[*endorsement*]
Understanding this to be substantially an order of General McClellan's, let it be executed at once.

> *A. Lincoln*

December 4, 1861

Harbinson, writing to Samuel Colt on December 7th, outlined the bitter struggle, saying that Berdan had been fighting the matter for the past six weeks. "Colonel B[erdan] says that Ripley is determined that the rifles shall not be ordered and General Marcy and himself are just as determined that they shall be ordered." If they failed in this attempt, said Harbinson, Berdan would go directly to Congress and seek an appropriation. The key to the entire proposition, he continued, was having the 1,000 rifles available on the spot. Would Samuel Colt authorize same?[112]

Apparently so. With Marcy's, McClellan's, and Lincoln's favorable endorsement, powerful political leverage existed for purchase of the Colt rifles. During another month of bureaucratic sparring and delay while the new Secretary of War, Edwin Stanton, was confirmed and McClellan recovered from a sickness, Colt readied the revolving rifles, shipping them to Washington, D.C. for immediate delivery. Colt's gamble soon paid off. Due to the decisive influence of Abraham Lincoln an order was issued January 27, 1862 for the purchase of 1,000 Colt revolving rifle muskets for Berdan's men. The very next day the Colts were delivered. This was fortunate for Colt, as on January 29th Ripley wrote on the Colt order, "It does not appear that General McClellan wants these guns, and...I should not be disposed to recommend their purchase."[113]

The truth at last had become fully evident. Berdan had sought the Colts only as a political means to the desired end of getting approval for the actual breechloaders which he wanted — the Sharps rifles. Having completely succeeded in obtaining final approval for the breechloaders,

Berdan had additionally demanded the Sharps rifles and won. On the same date as the order for the Colt revolving rifle muskets were issued (January 27, 1862), Ripley placed an order with Sharps for 1,000 rifles expressly for Berdan's Sharpshooters. These, combined with the Colts, Ripley anticipated, would equip both sharpshooter regiments.

Ripley soon found out that Berdan also demanded Sharps for the 2d regiment, hence his endorsement of January 29th on the Colt order. It was too late, of course, to cancel this order. Colt had already delivered the revolving rifle muskets and Berdan persisted in keeping these Colts, since most of his men would otherwise remain unarmed for a lengthy period. On February 6, 1862, evidently after more futile complaining on Ripley's part, the Ordnance Department placed a second order with Sharps for another 1,000 rifles for Colonel Henry Post's 2d Sharpshooters.[114]

Actually, it appears that as a sort of accommodation with the Ordnance Department, once final approval for the breechloaders was given, Berdan accepted the Army's standard cost for Sharps rifles. Despite having petitioned in October, 1861 for double set triggers and the saber bayonet at a cost of $43.00 per rifle (50 cents more than the standard military rifle with single trigger and saber bayonet earlier purchased by the Army), Berdan did not balk at the actual contracted cost per rifle of $42.50. This only involved his accepting the angular bayonet in place of the saber bayonet, while obtaining the highly desirable double set triggers. [The difference in respective costs is explained in the Sharps price list: $2.75 is shown as the cost of double set triggers, plus $2.50 for the angular bayonet and scabbard = $5.25; the standard saber bayonet and scabbard was $5.00 plus 75 cents for the bayonet stud on the barrel = $5.75; difference of 50 cents. Reference: The Company Clerk, p. 65, 66]

The final order was thus in place by early February, 1862. The Sharps rifles to be furnished per Berdan's specification would be 2,000 special order New Model 1859 military rifles fitted with angular bayonets and double set triggers at $42.50 each. Ripley, who had been outdone by the upstart New York colonel, continued to be very angry over this matter and appears to have been further embarrassed when he belatedly learned that the standard Sharps military rifle was not being purchased. In early March, 1862 he found out that the sharpshooter colonel was directly corresponding with Sharps about their configuration, and he bitterly complained to Secretary of War Stanton. In a nasty note to J.C. Palmer at Sharps, Ripley wrote on March 12th: "[Colonel Berdan] was not authorized to give you any instructions in relation to making the rifles. What ever variations you may have made at his insistence or his directions from the regular rifle ordered by the Dept. and whatever may be the effect of those variations, either in quantity, cost or time of delivery, must be at your own risk, and must be borne by you as to the consequence." Since there was no variation in cost between the standard and special order Sharps ($42.50), Berdan again was able to persevere. Yet the Sharps firm was busily expediting carbine production, including a special order for 343 carbines for the 2d Illinois Cavalry, and did not begin to convert their production to the Berdan rifles until about the first week in March, 1862.[115]

If Hiram Berdan thought his difficulties were over once the Sharps orders were placed, he was grossly mistaken. In fact the protracted struggle with Ripley seemed the least of his "gun difficulties" once the season for active campaigning approached in 1862.

Ironically, the source of the trouble was the very element he had utilized in winning his political victory over Ripley — the soon to be infamous Colt revolving rifle muskets.

When the Colts showed up in camp in early February, the 1st Sharpshooters refused to take them, preferring to wait for delivery of their Sharps — promised, said Captain Benjamin Giroux of Company C, "in twenty to twenty five days."

Colonel Post's 2d Sharpshooters, however, anticipating that they would be armed only after the 1st regiment's Sharps were delivered, accepted the Colts "until the Sharps can be made...."[116]

Once these Colts were examined and used, the 2d Sharpshooters were most unhappy. "Since we have got our Colts we have plenty of work to do," wrote a disgruntled sharpshooter in Company B, "it is as much work to take care of them as it would [be] to keep two pair of horses in good order...."

Additional companies who had been recruited throughout the fall and winter were arriving in camp expecting to be armed with the promised "superior rifles" that the recruiting ads had described in detail: "Sharps improved breech gate, cast steel barrels, patched ball [box], etc., made to order." They found only the Colts, which, "while pretty to look at," were "inaccurate and unreliable, prone to get out of order, and even dangerous to the user."[117]

Anonymous letters of complaint from the enlisted men about having been deceived on the gun issue began to show up in local newspapers, causing one officer of Company C, 1st Sharpshooters, to write in rebuttal that these men were being "growlers" without justification.[118]

This was merely the calm before the storm. With the approach of spring and active campaigning the men feared they had been "humbugged" about their promised Sharps, and would have to face the enemy with only the Colts and a few target rifles. On March 6, 1862, the matter spilled over in an ugly confrontation. Private Theodore Preston, of Company B, 2d U.S. Sharpshooters, described the events in breathless detail to his brother a few days later:

"Last Wednesday we had an order read on dress parade to be in readiness to march Saturday morning. So we all got our knapsacks packed and all things ready for a march. The officers flew around wonderful smartly; they thought that they saw themselves over the [Potomac] river in the smoke of battle, all mighty heroes. But in the meantime amid all the preparation for march[ing] some of the privates were scratching their noodle over a large sheet of paper, framing petitions to their respective [Congressional] Representatives stating how we were to be armed, and how we are armed, and the danger a person is in that fires one of the [Colt] guns, and the threats that were made to get us to take the guns, and the promises that were made us after we had them. That we were promised Sharps as soon as they could be made, and...now that we had learned the manual of arms we were to be rushed into battle with these poor guns, stating our dissatisfaction with the proceedings and praying them to do something for us. There were seven petitions sent in to as many Representatives.

"The result of all this was that these Representatives went to headquarters to see Major General McClellan, but he was absent and the Adjutant General suspended the order temporarily [for the sharpshooters to march] until McClellan should return and consider the matter, and confer with the Representatives. Then the Representatives came up here to see us and the guns. They said that they would do all for us that they could.

"They saw Colonel Berdan and had a talk with him. And you may guess that he was mad. He could hardly contain himself when he heard what had been done. It was very humiliating to him to think that he had been outgeneraled by the privates. When the commanding officers of

A Berdan Sharpshooter probably of the 2d regiment with his Colt revolving rifle musket ca. Feb./March, 1862. (collection Michael J. McAfee)

this regiment found out what had been done they were ready to split every private's head open. They called a meeting of the officers in the evening and had a hot time of it. The Colonel (Post), Lieut. Col. [Francis Peteler], Major [Amos B. Jones], and Adjutant [Lewis C. Parmelee] tried their prettiest to get the captains to resign. Two captains and one lieutenant did resign, and when they found that the others would not, they abused them as bad as they knew how [-] called them and their men cowards and everything else. The captains told them if they would stay in service six months that they would show them that they and their men were no cowards. The lieutenant colonel came down on [the] captain of Company A very hard [-] called him and his men everything. .....He [the captain] told the lieutenant colonel that if he would go out over the line with him he would show him that he weren't afraid of him nor two such men either.

"The Colonel (Post), and lieutenant colonel, major, adjutant, and quartermaster all sent in their resignations, with a provisionary clause in them that if they were not sent over the river soon that they would resign [outright]. Let them [if they] will, they have humbuged us about all they are going to. We have made up our minds to fight for our own rights first. When they do by us as they agreed to then we are ready to do battle for them. They have lied to us about long enough.

"The colonel says when he gives an order to march and the privates countermand it, that he thinks it time to resign. They are all acting in their respective positions yet, and I think that they will continue to act [so] until they are put out.

"Perhaps a slight description of the gun would not be out of the way. To commence with it is too light for the size and weight of lead [ball]. Second, when the ball leaves the cylinder and enters the barrel there are small shavings of lead [that] escape from between the cylinder and barrel and fly six or eight feet, endangering a person. Yes, I have often seen the boys picking out these pieces of lead from one another's necks and faces. Not long ago a fellow in Co. G was firing one when three barrels went off at once, cutting away his forefinger and thumb. The major was firing one not long since when it burst. All very true. But still they say it is a safe gun, and as good as they make. But if [the] Sharps is poorer we want it. For we think we are capable of judging a gun yet. If we are soldiers give us Sharps and we will run all the risk. For some unaccountable reason they will persist in our using and keeping these guns. But they have got a pill now that will set them a thinking. If they won't do anything for us,

why our Representatives will. And I think they will have as much influence as our officers.

"The officers are crestfallen to think that the privates should out wind them at last. Perhaps we are not through with it yet, but we are prepared for anything that comes up. What can't be cured must be endured. If they do out wind us...we may never get Sharps, nor another gun."[119]

Just as Private Preston had predicted, the men had, indeed, not heard the last on the matter. About ten days later he wrote another letter to his brother, reporting that the officers of the regiment had remained "raving mad." "To think that we privates were able to frustrate their designs was very humiliating to them. Their darling project has been to keep these [Colt] guns in our hands, for what reason I know not. Since those petitions were sent in they have been much more severe with the men [-] heavy marches with knapsacks packed and standing guard with them. They have worked many of the boys down sick."

Still the men of the 2d Sharpshooters remained firm in their resolve. Said Private Preston: "...if in this move we fail to get our Sharps Rifles we never will get them. I presume we will have a different gun before we go into action, if it is nothing more than a Springfield Rifled Musket, and those are preferable to these [Colts]."[120]

Hiram Berdan, of course, was not about to turn in the Colts, which would have been politically embarrassing beyond endurance. As it was, he had already appeared foolish following much publicity over what he referred to as "a state of mutiny on the gun question." While documentation is lacking, it appears he resolved the crisis by obtaining from Sharps and displaying to the sharpshooters that firm's representation that the desired Sharps rifles were then being manufactured and would soon be ready. By mid-March, however, the Sharps factory had only begun to change over their plant for rifle production. The last delivery of 500 carbines was made March 4th, and thereafter no deliveries of carbines occurred until May 31st (500). The Ordnance Department had been correct in believing the Berdan special order rifles would eliminate much Sharps carbine production — nearly three month's worth, as it turned out.[121]

On March 20, 1862 the 1st and 2d U.S. Sharpshooters were ordered to proceed to the war zone in Virginia. In the 1st regiment their surly mood was reflected by the statement of Rudolph Aschmann, who wrote: "Now everything was done to arm us at least with Colt guns (five chambered firearms constructed in the manner of revolvers with rifled barrels).

However our regiment insisted on its demand [of Sharps rifles].... On March 20, we, too, left Washington without guns." The 2d Sharpshooters had swallowed their pride, however, and went to war with the disliked Colts, fully expecting that they would be rearmed with the Sharps within a few weeks. Then, within a matter of days the 1st Sharpshooters changed their minds, and decided to take the Colts rather than remain largely unarmed. Said Aschmann: "Being in enemy land without arms was finally beginning to offend our sense of honor. Our Sharps rifles had not yet arrived, but we were assured that they would soon be in our hands. We therefore decided, although reluctantly, to accept the...Colt rifles."[122]

Mindful of the uneasy rumblings in both regiments about the Colts following the March 6th "mutiny," Berdan had continually badgered government officials and Sharps executives about obtaining delivery of his Sharps rifles. Apparently his urgent early March correspondence with Sharps had resulted in the company informing the Ordnance Department of a delay due to manufacturing so many special feature options (double set triggers), which led to Ripley's outburst on March 12th about extra costs and delayed deliveries. Once on the Virginia peninsula Berdan continued to write letters with furious abandon. Evidently not expecting much help from the Ordnance Department, he concentrated on petitioning various administration officials when it appeared the Ordnance Department was dragging their feet on inspecting and forwarding the arms.

Actually, the state of disorganization within the Ordnance Department in processing inspection of the 2000 special order Berdan Sharps rifles is fully evident in their correspondence files. On March 13th Ripley had telegraphed to Captain George T. Balch at the Springfield, Mass. Armory to inspect and forward all Sharps rifles then ready on the Berdan order. Balch learned on the same day that no rifles were then ready, nor would they soon be. He telegraphed a lengthy report on March 15th, and awaited further instructions from Ripley, stating that since Major Robert H.K. Whiteley had control of inspection at the Sharps factory he did not feel authorized to take further action in the matter.

When Ripley was further harassed on the as yet undelivered Sharps three weeks later, he telegraphed an inquiry to Captain Balch at Springfield (on April 5th), implying that Balch had forsaken this matter.

Balch, now aware that it was Ripley's "intention that I should take up and forward these arms," on April 6th assigned "one of the most energetic and competent inspectors I have" to inspect and forward these rifles "with utmost dispatch." This man was U.S. sub inspector John Taylor, then present at Springfield, but who was soon to be a major inspector of Colt revolvers in the same city, Hartford, Connecticut.

Because Major Whiteley, then at Sharps, had only two sub inspectors to examine arms for which four men appeared needed, Balch would not utilize Whiteley's men and told Taylor to take all the Colt inspectors needed to rush this work through. Balch's formal instructions to Taylor were written the following day:

Springfield, Mass.
April 7, 1862

Mr. John Taylor
U.S. Sub Inspector,
Hartford, Ct.
Sir.

In compliance with my verbal instructions given you yesterday you will proceed to take charge of the inspection of a lot of two thousand Sharps rifles for the Berdan Sharpshooters now making by the Sharps P.F.A.M. Co.

You will for this purpose take all the experienced inspectors you need from the force now at Colts Armory regardless for the time being of the delay that it may occasion there, their places to be filled by five men whom I shall direct to report to you within a day or two.

As these arms are most pressingly needed at this moment, and as the company are far behind their promised time of delivery, you will for a few days until you can overtake the manufacture, only look at the most important parts with strictness, such as the rifling and the lock.

Mr. Palmer reported yesterday by telegraph that the accouterments and ammunition had all gone forward and that 100 rifles would be ready to ship today and 70 a day hereafter.

If you find this to be the case, take all the men you need from Colts tomorrow and put the 100 through in a day & catch up as quickly as you can, shipping them as directed in my letter to Mr. Palmer, a copy of which I enclose for your information.

Do not give the company any ground to say that we delayed the shipments.

Respectfully,
Your obedient Servant,
Geo. T. Balch

Capt. Ord. Corps Inspector

Balch was much embarrassed, he told Ripley, for not even having a copy of the Sharps contract for these rifles, and on the same day, April 7th, requested same.[123]

John Taylor, who had hastened to Hartford, was soon being pressed by Brigadier General Ripley for reports. On April 23rd he sent the following letter to Ripley: "I received your telegraph this day and replied by telegraph. I now send you the number of [Sharps] rifles forwarded to Lt. T[homas] G. Baylor [Fortress Monroe, Va. Ordn. Officer] and the dates of the same:

April 11th	100
"	14	100
"	16	100
"	19	100
"	21	100
"	23	100

I have notified Capt. Balch at Springfield of the date of each 100 at the time they were forwarded and have sent him the certificates of 500 according to his order."[124]

It will be seen from the above that Sharps, despite their optimistic earlier estimates, was producing only about 50 rifles per day once the initial rifle delivery was made, which was 37 days after the final carbine delivery of March 4th. Indeed, recorded factory deliveries (in lots of 500) for the entire Berdan special order were reported as follows:

April 21, 1862 500
May 2, 1862 500
May 14, 1862 500
May 24, 1862 500

These rifles were shipped daily from the factory as received and inspected, directly to Lt. Baylor at Fortress Monroe, but due to shipment by steamer in random lots depending upon the availability of a ship, they arrived in segments. Berdan received the first lot, 600 rifles (the April 23rd production total) on May 7, 1862 while at Yorktown, Va.[125]

Immediately there was further trouble. On May 8th an angry Berdan began telegraphing to everyone involved in the project, including Ripley, J.C. Palmer, D.D. Tompkins [U.S. Quartermaster at New York], and E. N. Stebbins [Military Storekeeper, Washington, D.C. Arsenal]. It seems at long last he had his Sharps rifles, but they were useless without ammunition. As Berdan explained to Stebbins: "I received your invoice for 200,000 rounds of ammunition for Sharps Rifles some three weeks since. Neither Lieut. Baylor nor Quartermasters, nor Ordnance officers at Fortress Monroe or on the York River here have heard anything of it. I have examined nearly or all[most] all the vessels in the river & can get no trace of it." To J.C. Palmer at Sharps, Berdan was even more blunt: "I have 600 Sharps rifles but no ammunition. To whom & through whom & where did you send it. How much in ammunition have you got on hand that you could send today. Answer. H. Berdan, Col. Cmdg."[126]

Ironically, Sharps had forwarded the ammunition and appendages prior to April 7th, before the first shipment of rifles. Ripley notified Berdan by telegram on May 8th that 200,000 Sharps cartridges had left Washington, D.C. on board the steamer *City of Richmond* on April 27th. Yet due to mishandling and delay the shipment was temporarily lost. By the afternoon of May 8th Berdan finally located the ammunition, and Company F, 1st Sharpshooters were the first to be issued the new arms that day. Throughout May and into early June issues of the Sharps were made as received. The 2d regiment was the last to be armed, taking most of their Sharps at Falmouth, Va. on June 16, 1862."[127]

"The Colt five shooters were turned in without regret," wrote a sharpshooter officer. "All's well that ends well" thought another sharpshooter, who noted their new Sharps "were all that we could have wished for. Besides being easy and quick to load in any position, they fired accurately even at great distances. They were easy to clean and keep in good working order, and more than any other gun in the army they had the look of a weapon worthy of a sharpshooter." Soon this rifle came to be so well liked, said the man, "that even the companies which were equipped with target rifles exchanged the later for the new guns."[128]

Berdan who also was well pleased with the new Sharps rifles, did have the political wisdom to write in May, 1862 to Hugh Harbinson at Colt, telling him that the Colts were being turned in due to a "promise made to the men when they were enlisted that they should have the Sharps Rifles." Stating that "all my reputation thus far has been made with the Colts and the Target Rifles," the Colts had proved to be "a very superior weapon especially for skirmishers," said Berdan. Thus he was determined to keep them in the same Army Corps "if possible." Such, of course, proved to be only so much face saving rhetoric, and it appears that the unwanted Colts were shipped to the West, where many seem to have wound up in the hands of Michigan cavalrymen.[129] [Most of the 2d,

3d, and 4th Michigan Cavalry carried .56 caliber revolving rifle muskets from mid 1862 until 1864.][130]

Just how pleased the Berdan Sharpshooters were to have their Sharps is reflected in their subsequent comments about being able to lie prone, reload without changing position, and fire so rapidly as to drive away any but an overwhelming attacking enemy column. The velocity of the .52 caliber Sharps ball was such that when a member of Company K fired into an enemy held rifle pit at Kelly's Ford the bullet struck one man in the head, passed completely through, and lodged in another man's torso, killing both. A Confederate explained that he could tell from the sound of the bullets whistling overhead if the Yankees were using breechloaders. The "forced ball" from the breechloader was a little larger than the diameter of the rifle bore, and kept the propelling gasses from escaping around the ball, which provided greater velocity. If it were a breechloader, said the wary Confederate, "the bullet got to you before the report, but if it was a muzzle loader the report got to you before the ball." On the picket line after Fredricksburg, the outgunned Confederates arranged an uneasy truce with their opposite numbers, a detachment of Berdan Sharpshooters. "We knew it was you when you first began to shoot," said a Rebel, who admitted the Green Coats' Sharps rifles "were too sharp for them," and they would fire no more without giving notice.[132]

Comparatively light, well balanced, rugged in design, and simple in their mechanical function, the Sharps proved to be an outstanding success with the men. Their safety, in comparison with the Colt revolving rifle, was pronounced. "I never knew of an accident occurring by the premature discharge of a Sharps rifle," wrote a veteran captain after the war. California Joe, before he left the sharpshooters, outfitted himself with a new double set triggered Sharps, and even the sharpshooter officers were frequently found using these weapons in combat.

Particularly pleasing to the men were some of the features of their new rifles. The Sharps was equipped with a self contained pellet primer system, actuated by cocking and releasing the hammer. Although somewhat unreliable — "frequently failing to explode the cartridge" — they were a handy adjunct especially in freezing cold weather when it was difficult to place a regular percussion cap on the nipple. Further, when

As is suggested by leather leggings, ostrich feather plumed hat, and his double set triggered Sharps rifle, this is a Berdan Sharpshooter, ca. 1862. (Richard F. Carlile Coll.)

necessary to disable a rifle (such as to prevent its use when in danger of being captured by the enemy) a sharpshooter could quickly remove the breech block by taking out a single pin. The breech block then might be carried off or thrown away, rendering the rifle useless to an enemy. The stock, which contained a metal patch box, was not only a handy receptacle for spare percussion caps and cleaning tools, but on at least one occasion saved a sharpshooter from serious injury when an enemy bullet struck at this location.

Otherwise, these rifles were found practical for a variety of purposes. When Lieutenant Colonel Caspar Trepp was mortally wounded at Mine Run, a litter of Sharps rifles was fashioned to carry him from the battlefield. Too, the Sharps made a handy crutch if needed for a wounded man to hobble from the firing line. Even their often unused angular bayonets served as a good means to keep a tourniquet tight. Also, when the Sharps was found wanting there often seemed to be a way to overcome the deficiency. Because the rear sight was graduated only to 800 yards, a detail of sharpshooters cut small sticks to fit to the sight in order to increase the elevation while at the Po River in 1864. Their shots at an estimated 1,500 yards distance caused a Confederate signal station to be abandoned, reported an observer.[133]

Only one significant drawback was evident in the utilization of these Sharps rifles. As the sharpshooters soon learned, the greater rate of fire with their new rifles meant that they often had to carry a larger quantity of ammunition. While sixty rounds was standard (compared to the forty rounds for the .58 caliber muzzle loader), on certain occasions they carried many more, such as at Gettysburg. Too, there were engagements where their ammunition was quickly expended, and due to their non-standard .52 caliber linen cartridges, they could not be easily resupplied. At Malvern Hill in 1862 the sharpshooters had to be pulled from the battle, being out of ammunition.[134]

At the time the Berdan Sharpshooters were originally armed with the new Sharps rifles in May and June, 1862 their combined strength had dwindled to little more than 1,000 men. Because 2,000 rifles were available, and some of the men continued to carry target rifles, a substantial surplus of the double set triggered Sharps existed. These rifles were soon placed in the Washington, D.C. Arsenal, expressly for Berdan's exclusive use in replacing lost or damaged arms, and also for new recruits.

Yet with these highly desirable Sharps in idle inventory at the Washington Arsenal, and demands continually being made for first class small arms by disgruntled regimental commanders, the usurpation of Berdan's special order rifles was inevitable. Following Bull Run II and just prior to Antietam, Hiram Berdan learned that many of his rifles were missing from the arsenal, causing him to write an angry letter to division headquarters, demanding return of his misappropriated Sharps.

Washington D.C.
Sept. 16th 1862

[Major Frank S. Earle, A.A.A.G.]
Major,

I have the honor to report that on inquiry at the Ordnance Office on my arrival here, I found that not only all of the new Sharpes Rifles made expressly for my Command and needed for the recruits now coming into my Regt., but the guns that I had turned in for transportation from Harrison's Landing, by order of the Comdg. Genl. had been issued to other Regts. leaving me not a single Sharpes Rifle for my men returning from Hospitals or for my recruits.

I at once applied at Head Qrs. Army of the Potomac for an extension of my pass to enable me to recover at least a portion of my arms at once. I procured the extension and after much trouble succeeded in getting back 300 rifles from the Col. of a Mich. Regt. [probably the 16th Michigan Infantry] and 197 which I had turned in at Fortress Monroe. I have about 650 still out, which are in the hands of the Bucktails [13th Pennsylvania Reserves — 42d Pennsylvania Volunteer Infantry], and I must have them for the recruits and Companies which are coming into my Command under the recent call. Fifty (50) recruits for my Regt. have just arrived and more are on the way. I shall have them all armed and equipped here before they leave for the Regt.

Mr. Watson, Asst. Secy. of War, is very much annoyed at the way in which the Bucktails got my Sharpes Rifles from him, and says I have only to apply to Gen. McClellan and set forth the facts and he will order them to be returned to the Arsenal. The facts are these. Before marching from Harrison's Landing I received orders to turn in all extra arms for transportation. I turned in about 100 that belonged to men then in Hospitals. These guns were given to some Bucktails that had as I am informed just returned from Richmond [exchanged prisoners], of course without arms. On their arrival here their officers represented to Mr. Watson that their Regt. was partly armed with Sharpes Rifles and that there were enough at the Arsenal to arm the entire Regt. and they would like to have the Regt. all armed with them. Mr. Watson not knowing but the first really belonged to the Bucktails or that those at the Arsenal belonged to me and had been promised to my recruits, gave the Bucktails enough to arm the whole Regt. You will remember that in my call for recruits I stated that I had the Sharpes Rifles on hand. I am in an awkward situation not only with the recruits, but with the real owners of the guns which were turned in, as they are now many of them rejoining the Regt. and of course want their guns again.

   I have the honor to ask that Genl. McClellan will order these guns to be returned to the Arsenal at once. Mr. Watson says he will give the Bucktails Springfield Rifles instead. .....
Very Respectfully

Your Obdt. Servt.
H. Berdan
Col. Comdg. U.S.S.S. [135]

The day after Berdan wrote this letter the bloody battle of Antietam severely thinned the ranks of the 2d Sharpshooters and there were less than 500 enlisted men present for duty in both regiments. Despite the addition of at least fifty new recruits in late September it is doubtful that Berdan needed the additional rifles thereafter. Sullivan Cook, one of the new recruits assigned to Company I, 1st S.S., was issued his Sharps from the Washington Arsenal on September 22d. [136]

It is easy to understand Berdan's concern about losing the surplus Sharps. Company L of the 2d Sharpshooters had departed with perhaps 100 of these Sharps rifles when they joined the 1st Minnesota Infantry in mid 1862 (30 were listed in their possession as of Dec. 31, 1862). Yet two companies of the Andrew Sharpshooters [1st and 2d Companies, Massachusetts Sharpshooters], originally raised for Berdan's 2d regiment but serving as independent companies under the name derived of their state governor, John A. Andrew, had been offered Sharps rifles by Berdan in mid 1862. Despite the obvious advantages in firepower and mobility they had declined, preferring to keep their heavy barreled target rifles. At Antietam the 1st Company, serving with the 2d Corps, lost 26 men, their cumbersome target rifles "being little better...than clubs" in hand to hand fighting. The Andrew Sharpshooters thus "saw the light." By the first quarter 1863 their ordnance report tallied 11 target rifles and

---

Looking at the cameraman much as he would an armed Rebel, this unidentified sharpshooter with the open breechblock on his d.s.t. Sharps seems about as mean an individual as Company A had to offer. (Herb Peck, Jr. Coll.)

18 Sharps rifles for the 1st Company, and 32 Sharps rifles for the 2d Company. These Sharps undoubtedly were available Berdan model rifles, obtained from the Washington, D.C. Arsenal. [137]

The Pennsylvania Bucktails, despite Berdan's protest, continued to keep their surplus Berdan Sharps rifles. On August 9, 1862 that regiment had attempted to turn in their well used Enfields and Springfield rifle muskets, but had been offered only "inferior" arms, probably of foreign manufacture. Their colonel, Hugh W. McNeil adamantly marched his men back to camp and the next day was able to arrange for issue of the Sharps. On August 10th the 42d Pennsylvania "Bucktails" drew the Sharps, which were an immediate favorite. "They had round barrels, were of good carrying power and of extreme accuracy, were furnished with extra hair triggers [double set triggers], and could be fired with either caps or fulminating tapes," wrote the Bucktail historian. Later, when the regiment was rearmed with Spencer rifles in mid 1864, many of the Pennsylvanians continued to regard the Sharps as superior. One disgruntled Bucktail, when ordered to turn in his Sharps for a Spencer, smuggled it out of camp and succeeded in shipping it home where it remained a highly prized item forty years later. The actual quantity of Berdan Sharps appropriated by the Bucktails may have been substantially less than the 650 rifles stated by Berdan. Their 4th quarter (December 31), 1862 ordnance report shows 140 Sharps rifles in the hands of eight companies, one company not reporting, and another (Co. H) absent and armed with Model 1842 .69 caliber muskets. [138]

With heavy losses in personnel among Berdan's Sharpshooters due to combat and sickness, so many surplus Sharps rifles remained on hand in March, 1863 that the entire sharpshooter "brigade" was reissued new or refurbished weapons that month. Issues of replacement Sharps to the 1st U.S. Sharpshooters at Falmouth, Va. on March 31, 1863 were as follows: [139]

Company A	36
Company B	57
Company C	58
Company D	16
Company E	28
Company F	59
Company G	58
Company H	38
Company I	39

were 10 nipple cones, and 10 primer springs. While the excellent durability of the Sharps is thus indicated by these nominal minor repairs (continuing the rifle in active service), a list of the spare parts maintained by the armorer shows the extent to which a Sharps could be reworked before being sent to the divisional ordnance officer for armory refurbishing.

16 triggers	20 middle bands
4 hammers	78 band springs
23 levers	10 lock plates
4 receivers	38 cones
30 mainsprings	7 front sight studs

plus other miscellaneous Sharps parts[141]

Of course, the rifles were but one item in the overall list of equipment utilized by each company. As reported by Captain F. E. Marble for the period ended March 31, 1862, the typical inventory of Company G, 1st U.S.S.S. consisted of the following items:

57 Sharps rifles
58 Sharps rifles
52 bayonets and scabbards
56 body [waist] belts
23 cross belts
26 "U.S." belt plates
58 cartridge boxes
58 cap boxes
50 swab brushes
1 swab stick
38 rifle slings

Damage to leather items from active service was so severe in the sharpshooters that large quantities of the Sharps related accouterments had to be periodically replaced. Lieutenant Colonel Trepp sent the following items from Culpeper, Va. to Washington, D.C. September 23, 1863, being turn ins due to damage in active service:[142]

272 bayonet scabbards
56 cap pouches

Enlargement of the double set triggered Sharps rifle in the hands of California Joe (see illustration in part II). Note Joe's incongruent angular bayonet fitted rifle and his original saber bayonet for the single triggered private weapon he purchased in Washington, D.C. in 1861. Joe's single trigger Sharps was disabled on the Peninsula, and he evidently reequipped himself for the photograph from the Washington Arsenal in Sept., 1862. (courtesy Vermont Historical Society)

130 cartridge boxes
12 ctg. box belts and plates
14 waist belts and plates
10 triangular bayonets
1 arms chest

Few of the special order Sharps "Berdan Sharpshooters" model rifles are believed to have remained in active service following the breakup of the sharpshooter organization in late 1864 and early 1865. Worn and well used, many were deposited in the Federal arsenals for storage until ultimately sold as surplus for a few dollars each. In 1865 a total of 3,454 Sharps rifles were privately purchased by returning Union soldiers at a cost of $8.00 each. These figures included New Model 1863 rifles, 6,150 of which were delivered to the U.S. Army from March 21st to June 30, 1865. In all a total of 9,350 Sharps rifles had been purchased by the Army during the war, 8,270 of which were direct from the Sharps firm. The most important of these, by far, had been the 2,000 special order double set trigger rifles made for the Berdan Sharpshooters in April and May, 1862.[143]

As Captain Charles A. Stevens wrote after the war: "It was owing to the success attained by the Berdan Sharpshooters in developing the superiority of the Sharps breech-loading rifle...that caused so soon after the war the substitution of the breech loading system...in all manner of firearms." Stevens' comments, while of questionable accuracy considering the performance of units using the Henry and especially Spencer metallic cartridge firing breechloaders during the war, provided a fair measure of the enormous success of the Berdan special order Sharps rifles. Today these Sharps surely rank as among the most historic and significant of American firearms, and considering their relative rarity, are a true collector's treasure.[144]

Sharps New Model 1859, Berdan Special Order, Breechloading Rifle, serial no. 56113. Fitted with double set triggers, and equipped for the angular bayonet. Supplied on the Berdan contracts of Jan. 27, 1862, and Feb. 6, 1862. Note the unusual higher grade burl walnut stock — with martial inspectors marks on the reverse stock at the wrist — not normally found on a military arm. This suggests that the Sharps factory was hard pressed to quickly fill the entire Berdan special order, which required 2,000 military grade rifle stocks, without utilizing some hand seasoned civilian sporting rifle stocks. Because of the slot for the carbine sling bar, stocks prepared for carbine production were not adaptable to the military rifle. (author's collection)

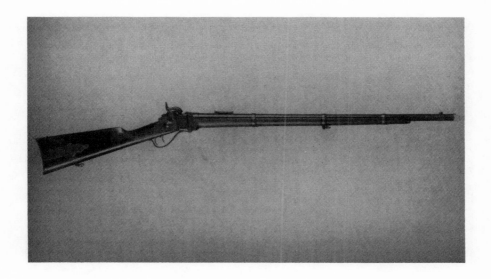

BERDAN SHARPS RIFLES — COLLECTOR'S PROFILE

Description: This rifle was the standard Sharps New Model 1859 military rifle with a few exceptions: 1) It was fitted for the angular socket bayonet which utilized the front sight stud to lock in place, no separate locking lug being present on the bottom of the barrel near the muzzle, as for the saber bayonet. 2) The rifle was fitted with a double set trigger mechanism, which by first pulling the rear trigger, set the forward "hair" trigger so that the slightest of pressure would release the hammer. Due to the special configuration, no lever locking latch was present on the trigger tang to hold the lever closed, as with single trigger rifles.

The standard features of the rifle were straight type breech design, back action lock with exposed S shaped hammer and pellet primer system, thirty inch round barrel, marked "Sharps Rifle/ Manufg. Co./ Hartford Conn." in three lines forward of the rear sight, and "New Model 1859" near the breech. Rear sights are found graduated to either 700 or 800 yards. Three spring held type oval barrel bands are utilized to hold the forestock in place. The metal furniture of the rifle, including buttplate, sling swivels, and spring hinged patchbox are of iron. The receiver and stock are not drilled or slotted to receive a sling bar, which was utilized on carbines only. Serial numbers are stamped on the upper stock tang and bottom of the barrel. Army inspector's initials are found on the

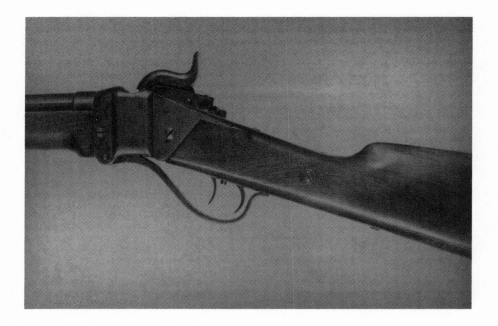

Reverse view of Sharps rifle #56113. Martial inspector's cartouche (JT), for John Taylor, is visible on the upper wrist of the stock. Per Ordnance Department records, John Taylor inspected all 2,000 Berdan special contract rifles between April 11th and May 24th, 1862. (author's collection)

reverse buttstock at the upper wrist (stamped cartouche), and often on the reverse side of the barrel at the breech (stamped initial or initials). Overall length of the rifle is forty-seven and one eighth inches, and the unloaded weight is eight pounds twelve ounces.

Army Inspector's Marks: John Taylor, aided by four or five civilian sub inspectors in the Army's employ who were borrowed from the Colt factory, inspected all 2,000 of the special order Berdan Sharps rifles between April 10th and May 24th 1862. John Taylor's right hand slant cartouche with the scroll initials "J T" was stamped on all original buttstocks. His initial "T" has been observed on some barrels in the normal army inspector's location at the breech. Since Taylor had several other employees working for him (including Colt sub inspector Orville W. Ainsworth, later the noted sub inspector of the first contract Colt Model 1873 Single Action Army Revolver), the presence of other initials would not be unusual on the barrel, if marked "New Model 1859." Arms received by the Army in 1865 on the last contract show different inspectors' initials, including "EAW" and "TWR" on the stock.[146]

Serial Numbers: Serial Numbers can provide significant information about a potential Berdan Sharps rifle, yet as a sole indicator they may be misleading and should not be regarded as an absolute when assessing a Berdan contract arm. Because the Sharps firm utilized a consecutive serial numbering system inclusive of all rifles and carbines manufactured regardless of model, it is logical that the Berdan Sharps rifles are to be found with numbers in the general sequence for March through May, 1862 production. Yet beyond this the Sharps firm certainly did not have the collector or historian in mind when numbering and shipping their weapons.

Sharps utilized the sub contract system in their factory, whereby batch production of arms by each individual contractor often resulted in out of chronological production sequence by serial number. Serial numbers were assigned to a given lot during the finishing and assembly stages of production. The contractors worked within the Sharps building and hired their own help to manufacture a lot or batch quantity of arms. Because of the varying speed of the individual contractors in completing their work a frequent variation in completion date was noted, and thus chronologically out of serial number shipping sequences. From the fragment of surviving Sharps serial number records for the Civil War era (serial numbers beginning in the 79,000 range, in the Connecticut State Library) it is apparent that days, months, and occasionally almost a year elapsed between shipping dates of consecutively numbered arms. As an example, these records show carbine no. 79116 delivered to the Army April 29, 1863, while no. 79117 was delivered February 20, 1864; #83671 delivered July 13, 1863, #83672 delivered Feb. 20, 1864; #83688 delivered June 25, 1863, #83689 delivered July 13, 1863. The normal current serial number to current shipment ratio was about 80%, based upon a random selection of records. Of numbers 79101 to 79150 thirty one were shipped April 21 — April 30, 1863, and eleven in May, 1863, (84% current ratio). For the fifty carbines in the 83651 — 83700 series, forty were shipped in the June — July, 1863 period (80% current ratio). Accordingly, within the serial ranges associated with Berdan contract, many numbers on rifles toward the end of and slightly higher than the estimated ranges appear to have been shipped at a later date (probably 1865), based upon the presence of Army inspector's marks other than John Taylor's (and his known sub inspectors). The reason for an 1862 period serial number on a much later delivered arm, of course, would relate to a slight overproduction at the Sharps factory in 1862, allowing for Army inspectors' rejections, and/or possible future Ordnance Department orders for these rifles. After the Berdan special order only 20 Sharps rifles (fitted for saber bayonets) were shipped from the factory to the Army (purchase of March 11, 1863) prior to the large scale 1865 deliveries (beginning with 150 triangular bayonet rifles on February 6, 1865). Thus any surplus 1862 manufactured rifles bearing corresponding serial numbers appear to have remained in inventory for an extended period before being inspected and shipped.[147]

Of further complication in isolating the Berdan serial numbers was the discovery that Sharps carbines were numbered among the sequence of rifle numbers for correct description Berdan rifles. In fact, of the primary serial number spread of approximately 3184 numbers noted for the Berdan configuration rifles, only 2000 rifles were made and delivered. Accordingly, about one in three Sharps arms in the Berdan number sequence are carbines. Because of the integration of rifle production while carbine manufacture was still in process, the serial numbers assigned during the finishing stage were at random according to type of arm as a result of the batch system. Due to the subsequent restoration of carbine production while the last of the Berdan special order rifles were being processed, the batch effect again is perceived to have resulted in some out of sequence numbering.

Nonetheless, by estimating rate of production, and factoring in known deliveries from recorded Ordnance records, then working backward from the fragments of factory shipping ledger data extant, a reasonable estimate for the March — May, 1862 Sharps serial ranges was derived. These numbers were in the mid 50000 serial number range. When compared with the numbers of surviving correct configuration Sharps Berdan model rifles it was apparent this estimate was accurate. Subsequently, a significant number of documented Berdan Sharps serial numbers were discovered in original records, providing full confirmation that the Berdan special order was generally numbered as estimated. Although individual variations are possible, and certainly the last word has not been written on the subject, it appears the following is accurate with regard to the Berdan serial numbers.

There appear to be two separate serial ranges that exist for correct configuration Sharps Berdan special order rifles.

1) approximately 39573 to 40872

This is the secondary range, believed to have involved only a very few existing rifles which were on hand at the beginning of the Berdan contract, and were utilized to fill the pressing demand for these arms. Accordingly they originally may have been single trigger rifles which were reequipped with double set triggers. While various rifles exist in this and adjacent ranges, very few have been shown to be originally of the correct d.s.t. profile, and bearing "J T" inspector's marks. No documented arms exist in this range, and it is estimated that less than 25 rifles of this approximate number sequence may have been involved in the Berdan contract.

2) 54390 — 57574

This is the primary Berdan Sharps estimated serial range. All of the documented arms thus far known, as well as nearly all of the correct description rifles are found in this sequence. Certain carbines, as mentioned above, fall within this range, including many in the low 55300 sequence (ie: #55305, #55354). The actual Berdan Sharpshooter documented numbers suggest that these rifles were issued randomly, and no correlation with serial number exists as to unit of issue. Both the 1st and 2d U.S. Sharpshooters are known to have carried rifles in the 54000, 55000, 56000, and 57000 serial ranges. Accordingly, those Berdan Sharps issued subsequently to the Andrew Sharpshooters, Co. L of the 1st Minnesota, and the Pennsylvania Bucktails (42d Pa. Vol. Inf.) are believed to be similarly randomly numbered within the above estimated range. Certain Sharps rifles of slightly higher numbers than #57574 may have some possibility of association with the Berdan Sharpshooters. Because of the rush to complete the Berdan special order it is possible that a few rifles at the tail end of production went out without the double set triggers, which were very time consuming to make. At least one rifle of single trigger type has been reported with John Taylor inspector marks (#57743). This may involve a replacement stock or trigger mechanism, and until further evidence is presented no final conclusion seems possible on this aspect. It should be remembered, however, that most Sharps triangular bayonet rifles with single triggers in the high 57000 and lower 58000 serial number range were 1865 delivered arms, and thus are not

Enlargement of California Joe and his Sharps (see illustration in Part II), showing the muzzle of the rifle which is of the angular bayonet profile — without locking lug on the bottom of the barrel. (courtesy of the Vermont Historical Society)

associated with the Berdan contract.[148]

Is it a Berdan Sharps? Generally, the one constant premise in evaluating a possible Berdan Sharps rifle is its inspection by John Taylor. Bear in mind that other inspector's initials may appear on the barrel, such as "O W A," for O. W. Ainsworth, brought over from Colt as sub inspector. A list of documented and surviving correct profile Sharps Berdan model rifles is listed below, along with other Sharps rifles of some relevance as a reference aid. The numbers provided and remarks made do not guarantee the originality or authenticity of any item. They are in most cases rifles that have been reported, and have not been personally observed.

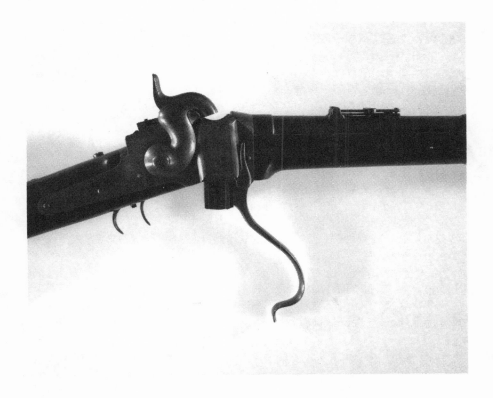

Detailed view of the back action lock and double set trigger mechanism of a Berdan contract Sharps rifle, serial no. 54580. (Andrew Mowbray Coll.)

Only those rifles where certain features were indicated (such as type of trigger, inspector's marks, etc.)have been included.

Documented Sharps Berdan Sharpshooters Rifles

From original source material, including regimental records, diaries, and correspondence.

#54858 Received Nov. 15, 1862, for Co. G, 1st S.S. R. Foster, armorer [Trepp Papers, N.Y. Hist. Soc.]

#55085 Found in camp Nov. 1, 1862 [Record book, 1st S.S. in National Archives, Record Group 94]

#55820 Issued to Co. G, 1st S.S., Nov. 12, 1862 [Trepp Papers, N.Y.

Hist. Soc.]LL

#56371 Rec'd from Henry Poribrin [?] Co B, 1st S.S. Nov. 21, 1862 [Trepp Papers N.Y. Hist. Soc.]

#56438 Issued to Pvt. Wm. Greene, Co. G, 2d S.S. in 1864[Diary of Wm. B. Greene, Wiley Sword collection]

#56793 Issued to Pvt. Wm. Greene, Co. G, 2d S.S. July 7,1864 [Diary of Wm. B. Greene, Sword collection]

#56974 Issued to Co. G, 1st S.S., Nov. 15, 1862 [Trepp Papers, N.Y. Hist. Soc.]

#57131 Rec'd for Co. G, 1st S.S., no date, ca. 1862 H. W. Woodbery [Trepp Papers, N.Y. Hist. Soc.]

#57266 Rec'd for Co. G, 1st S.S., no date, ca. 1862 D. A. Beard [Trepp Papers, N.Y. Hist. Soc.]

#57386 Rec'd for Co. G, 1st S.S., no date, ca. 1862 W.C. Wittrey [Trepp Papers, N.Y. Hist. Soc.]

#57471 Rec'd for Co. G, 1st S.S., no date, ca. 1862 Geo. W. Griffin [Trepp Papers, N.Y. Hist. Soc.]

#57574 Rec'd for Co. G, 1st S.S., no date, ca. 1862 C.D. Howley [Trepp Papers N.Y. Hist. Soc.]

List of Surviving Sharps Berdan Rifles — Correct Profile

Sharps New Model 1859 military rifles, reported as having double set triggers, fitted for the angular bayonet, and inspected by John Taylor, [(JT) cartouche on reverse of stock at upper wrist].

39573	55008	56113	57029
54390	55058	56219	57141
54412	55066	56309	57290
54478	55074	56314	57567
54492	55094	56452b	
54538	55096	56507b,c	
54549	55154	56736	
54571	55396	56739	
54580	55397a	56799	
54610	55402	56850b	
54665	55817	56860	
54716	55942	56879	
54910	55968	56900	
54976	55990	56920	
54998			

a — reported with tag as recovered from Antietam battlefield by Quartermaster L.W. Muzzy, 12th Mass. Inf., Sept. 17, 1862
b — reported with "OWA" inspector's marks on barrel
c — reported as in the possession of Pvt. Alan T. Lawrence, 3d Georgia Vols., paroled Confederate soldier, exchanged Nov. 1862

List of Sharps Rifles — Relevant to the Berdan Special Order
Sharps military rifles of the Civil War period, showing alterations, 1862 sequence serial numbers, or significant features bearing on the Berdan Sharps contract.
#40872 — d.s.t., with saber bayonet lug, military inspector's marks. This is the profile believed to have been originally requested by Berdan in his letter of Oct. 22, 1861 — the $43.00 rifle.
#54728 — single trigger, "JT" inspected stock. Converted to .50/70 centerfire. Believed to have been an original Berdan rifle converted by the Army, including a replaced trigger assembly.
#54767 — replaced stock assembly, including single trigger.
#55047, #55948, #56176, #56293, #56344, #56775, #56781, #56904, #57106, #57361 — single trigger arms within the Berdan serial ranges; some apparently were refinished and reconditioned post war, others may be Berdan issues with field replacements of the d.s.t. trigger assembly, some may be rejections from the Berdan contract and sold later.
#57576 — this rifle has a single trigger, is fitted for the saber bayonet, the barrel is marked "New Model 1863," and was inspected by "TWR." It remains in near mint condition. This is believed to be a very rare example of the twenty arms shipped to the Army March 11, 1863.
#57743 — reported to have a single trigger, "JT" cartouche, and fitted for the angular bayonet. Perhaps one of the few non double set triggered Berdan Sharps.
#57695, #57864, #57881, #57938, #57980, #58104 — believed to be rifles initiated in the 1862 production sequence, but shipped at a later date (1865 for those with other military inspector's marks and fitted for the angular bayonet).

NOTES

Part I - Hiram Berdan: The Man

1. *New York at Gettysburg, Final Report on the Battlefield of Gettysburg,* vol. III, Albany, N.Y., 1900, p. 1079
2. Rudolph Aschmann, *Three Years in the Army of the Potomac, p. 37; War of the Rebellion; Official Records of the Union and Confederate Armies* (hereafter cited as O.R.). vol. 27, part 1, p. 517; William C. Kent, "Sharpshooting With Berdan," *Civil War Times, Illustrated,* May, 1976, p. 6.
3. William F. Fox, *Regimental Losses in the American Civil War, 1861-1865,* Albany, N.Y., 1898, p. 419.
4. C.A. Stevens, *Berdan's United States Sharpshooters in the Army of the Potomac, 1861-1865,* St. Paul, Minn., 1882, p. 526; *Detroit Daily Advertiser,* Aug. 22, 1861.
5. *Detroit Daily Advertiser,* Aug, 22, 1861.
6. Hiram Berdan, Military Service Records, National Archives, Washington, D.C.
7. Aschmann, op. cit., p. 29.
8. Stevens, op. cit., p. 3.
9. Stevens, p. 2.
10. Stevens, p. 3; Aschmann, p. 30; William Y.W. Ripley, *Vermont Riflemen in the War for the Union 1861-1865,* Rutland, Vt., 1883, pp. 9-10.
11. Berdan, Mil. Serv. Records, National Archives.
12. Stevens, pp. 6, 9-11; Aschmann, p. 38.
13. Aschmann, p. 37.
14. Stevens, pp. 23, 25.
15. Aschmann, pp. 36-37.
16. Stevens, p. 510; Aschmann, p. 40; Ripley, p. 13.
17. Stevens, p. 528.
18. Stevens, p. 7; Roy Marcot, *Spencer Repeating Firearms,* Irvine, Calif., 1983, p. 52; James L. Mitchell, Colt, the Man, the Arms, the Company, Harrisburg, Pa., 1959, pp. 256-259; Ripley, p. 12.
19. Inspection Report, 1st U.S. Sharpshooters, Dec. 19, 1862, Record Group 94, National Archives; Aschmann, pp. 38, 47, 50; Stevens, p. 6; Mitchell, p. 257.
20. Hiram Berdan, Court Martial Records, RG 153, LL 188, March 3, 1863, National Archives, Washington, D.C.
21. Berdan, court martial testimony, op. cit., March 3, 1863.
22. O.R., vol. 11, pt. 2, pp. 278-279.
23. O.R., vol. 11, pt. 2, p. 279; Berdan court martial testimony, March 3, 1863.
24. Berdan court martial testimony, March 3, 1863.
25. O.R., vol, 11, pt. 2, p. 301; Stevens, p. 43.
26. Stevens, p. 25.
27. Berdan court martial testimony, March 3, 1863; Berdan military service records, Na-

tional Archives.

28. Ibid.

29. Berdan court martial testimony, March 3, 1863.

30. Ibid.; Caspar Trepp Papers, Trepp to Hancock, Feb 1, 1863, New York Historical Society, Albany, N.Y.; Caspar Trepp, military service records, National Archives, Washington, D.C.; Aschmann, p. 107; Inspection Report, 1st U.S. Sharpshooters, Nov. 1, 1862, National Archives.

31. Aschmann, p. 107; Insp. Rept., 1st U.S.S.S., Dec. 19, 1862.

32. Sullivan Cook, letter of Dec. 27, 1862, University of Michigan, Bentley Historical Library, Ann Arbor; Caspar Trepp Papers, Trepp to Berdan, Dec. 26, 1862, N.Y. Hist. Soc.

33. Caspar Trepp Papers, Trepp to Berdan, Dec. 26, 1862, Feb. 12, 1863, N.Y. Hist. Soc.; Caspar Trepp, Court Martial Records, RG 153, LL 89, Feb. 19, 1863, National Archives.

34. O.R., vol. 21, p. 973; Stevens, p. 234.

35. Caspar Trepp, court martial testimony, Feb. 19, 1863; Hiram Berdan, court martial testimony, March 3, 1863.

36. Aschmann, p. 107; O.R., vol. 25, pt. 1, p. 162.

37. Stevens, pp. 248-251; Caspar Trepp Papers, George Hastings to Trepp, May 26, 1863, Weston to Trepp, May 11, 1863, N.Y. Hist. Soc.

38. Hiram Berdan, mil. serv. records, Nat. Archives; Richard A Sauers, "Sickles - Right or Wrong?" *Blue & Gray Magazine,* March, 1988, p. 59.

39. O.R., vol. 27, pt. 1, p. 482.

40. *New York at Gettysburg,* III, p. 1067; O.R., vol. 27, pt. 1, pp. 72, 482, 507, 514-517.

41. O.R., vol. 27, pt. 1, p. 517.

42. O.R., vol. 27, pt. 2, pp. 616-617.

43. O.R., vol. 27, pt. 1, pp. 507, 514-517; vol. 27, pt. 2, p. 617.

44. O.R., vol. 27, pt. 1, pp. 72, 116, 482, 507, 514, 592, 598.

45. Sauers, op. cit., pp. 13, 56ff.; *New York at Gettysburg,* III, p. 1079.

46. O.R., vol. 27, pt. 1, p. 517; Stevens, p. 313.

47. O.R., vol. 27, pt. 1, p. 514-517.

48. Hiram Berdan, mil. serv. records, Nat. Arch.; Edward A. Hull, "Berdan's Breechloaders," (in seven parts), *The Gun Report,* March, 1987 to December, 1987, [March, 1987, p. 14ff].

49. Hull, op. cit., parts 1-7; Stevens, p. 527.

50. Hiram Berdan, mil. ser. records, Nat. Arch.; Stevens, p. 527.

51. *New York at Gettysburg,* III, p. 1074.

Part II - Berdan's Sharpshooters - The Men

52. John Q. Imholte, *The First Volunteer, History of the First Minnesota Volunteer Regiment 1861-1865,* Minneapolis, 1963, pp. 98-99.

53. Aschmann, pp. 30,40; "Pierce's Sharpshooters" recruiting brochure, dated Columbus [Ohio], July 29, 1862.

54. *Detroit Tribune,* July 11,17, 1861; Caspar Trepp Papers, document, n/d, "T. Suter - Swiss Rifle," N.Y. Hist. Soc.; Imholte, op. cit., pp. 98-99; Stevens, p. 455.

55. Theodore Preston letter, Nov. 13, 1881, U. of Mich.; Aschmann, pp. 30-32.

56. Stevens, pp. 18, 20, 22, 24, 74; Aschmann, p. 41.

57. Stevens, pp. 12, 18-19.
58. Michael J. McAfee, "Sharpshooters, U.S. Army Uniforms of the Civil War," Part VII, *Military Images,* March/April, 1984, pp. 6-8; G. W. Smith letter, Feb. 11, 1862, priv. colln.
59. Stevens, pp. 16-19; Ripley pp. 14-15; Aschmann, p. 41.
60. Stevens, pp. 11-12; Aschmann, p. 107.
61. Caspar Trepp Papers, target practice records, Jan. 14, 1863, N.Y. Hist. Soc.
62. Aschmann, p. 30.
63. Theodore Preston letter, Feb. 22, 1862, U. of Mich.; Stevens, pp. 26-27.
64. Stevens, pp. 53, 57, 58, 162.
65. Stevens, p. 41; Ripley, p. 24.
66. Stevens, pp. 55-56, 62-64.
67. Stevens, pp. 27, 161.
68. Stevens, pp. 59, 60.
69. Stevens, pp. 75, 110, 122, 144-145, 163.
70. Stevens, p. 133; G.G. Benedict, op. cit., p. 737-738.
71. Stevens, pp. 81, 156-158; Aschmann, p. 34.
72. Stevens, pp. 15-16; Caspar Trepp Papers, 1st U.S.S.S. returns, Dec. 31, 1862, March 31, 1863, N.Y. Hist. Soc.; Inspection reports, 1st U.S.S.S., Nov. 1, 1862, Dec. 19, 1862, National Archives.
73. Caspar Trepp Papers, Trepp to Adj.Gen. L. Thomas, March 21, 1863, N.Y. Hist. Soc.
74. Stevens, p. 93; Imholte, pp. 98-99, 210.
75. *New York at Gettysburg,* III, p. 1072; Stevens, p. 399; Trepp Papers, Trepp to Berdan, May 31, 1863, N.Y. Hist. Soc.
76. Kent, "Sharpshooting With Berdan," op. cit., pp. 8, 46, 47.
77. Stevens, p. 190.
78. Stuart G. Vogt, "'California Joe' Head," *Military Images,* March/April, 1984, pp. 10ff; Stevens, pp. 39, 48-49, 138.
79. Stevens, pp. 62, 78, 90, 118, 134.
80. Stevens, pp. 31, 102, 237.
81. Stevens, pp. 106, 165, 235, 240.
82. Caspar Trepp Papers, Specifications Against C. Trepp, Aug. 24, 1863, N.Y. Hist. Soc.
83. Stevens, pp. 519ff.
84. Inspection reports, 1st U.S.S.S., Nov. 1, 1862, Dec. 19, 1862, Nat. Arch.
85. Sullivan Cook letters, Nov. 12, 1862, Jan. 5,12, 1863, U. of Mich.; Stevens, p. 211.
86. Hiram Berdan, court martial records, March 3, 1863, Nat. Arch.; Albert G. Austin letter, n/d [1863], Sullivan Cook collection, U. of Mich.
87. Stevens, pp. 46, 216, 428; Caspar Trepp Papers, J.B. Isler to Trepp, Sept. 24, 1862, N.Y. Hist. Soc.
88. Stevens, pp. 188-189, 202.
89. Stevens, pp. 244, 248-253, 264.
90. Stevens, p. 327; O.R., vol. 27, pt. 1, pp. 518-519, 624.
91. Stevens, pp. 349-350.
92. Stevens, pp. 272, 359; Caspar Trepp Papers, Report of Major George Hastings, May 26, 1863, N.Y. Hist. Soc.

93. Stevens, p. 394; William B. Greene diary, 1864, private colln.

94. Stevens, pp. 427-428, 447, 451.

95. Stevens, pp. 419, 456, 464, 486, 494.

96. Stevens, p. 489; Frederick H. Dyer, *A Compendium of the War of the Rebellion,* vol. III, pp. 1716-1717; *New York at Gettysburg,* III, p. 1075.

97. Stevens, pp. 311, 340.

98. Ripley, p. 199; Stevens, p. 550.

Part III - The Berdan Sharps Rifle

99. Sharps sales catalog, Nov. 1, 1959.

100. Mitchell, p. 259.

101. Ripley, p. 3.

102. Berdan to R.S. Lawrence, Sept. 21, 1861, telegrams, RG 107, M504, Roll 2, National Archives, Washington, D.C.

103. *Detroit Free Press,* Jan. 24, 1862 (1:2).

104. Berdan to Simon Cameron, Oct. 22, 1861, Record Book, 1st U.S. Sharpshooters, RG 94, National Archives.

105. Stevens, pp. 7, 39.

106. House of Representatives, Executive Document, v.12 no.99, (U.S. 1338), pp. 550ff.

107. Mitchell, pp. 255ff.

108. Theodore Preston letter, Nov. 13, 1861, U. of Mich.

109. Mitchell, pp. 255ff; R. L. Wilson, *The Colt Heritage,* N.Y.,1979, p. 148.

110. R.L. Wilson, op. cit., p. 145.

111. House of Representatives, Executive Document, no. 66, (U.S. 1131), pp. 30-31.

112. Mitchell, pp. 256-259.

113. *Detroit Free Press,* Jan. 8, 1862; Mitchell, pp. 259-260; John D. McAulay, *Civil War Breechloading Rifles,* Lincoln, R.I., 1987, p. 17.

114. H. of Rep., Ex. Doc., (U.S. 1338), p. 551.

115. H. of Rep., Ex. Doc., (U.S. 1338), pp. 352, 946; Ripley to J.C. Palmer, March 13, 1862, letters sent by the chief of ordnance, RG 156, miscl., v. 54, p. 553.

116. Aschmann, p. 47; G. W. Smith letter, Feb. 11, 1862, pvt. colln.; *Detroit Free Press,* Feb. 6, 1862 (1:6).

117. Theodore Preston letter, Feb. 22, 1862, U. of Mich.; *Detroit Free Press,* Nov. 8, 1861, (1:3); Ripley, p. 16.

118. Detroit Free Press, Feb. 6, 1862, (1:6).

119. Theodore Preston letter, March 10, 1862, U. of Mich.

120. Theodore Preston letter, n/d [ca. March 20, 1862], U. of Mich.

121. Inspection reports, 1st U.S. Sharpshooters, Nov. 1, 1862, Dec. 19, 1862, Nat. Arch.; H. of Rep., Ex. Doc. (U.S. 1338),p. 346.

122. Stevens, p. 26; Aschmann, pp. 47,50.

123. G.T. Balch to Ripley, April 7, 1862 (two letters), RG 156 E21 #468, #469, National Ardhives.

124. John Taylor to Ripley, April 23, 1862, RG 156, Letters Received, E 21, 1862, #393 T, National Archives.

125. H. of Rep., Ex. Doc., (U.S. 1338) p. 946; Ripley to C.P. Kingsbury, April 10, 1862, RG 156, Letters Sent, miscl., vol. 55, p. 57; Berdan to E.N. Stebbins, May 10, 1862, RG 107, telegrams, M 504, Roll 29, 1088-1106, Nat. Archives.

126. Berdan to miscl., May 8-10, 1862, RG 107, telegrams, M 504, Roll 29, 1088-1106, National Archives.

127. Ripley to Berdan, May 8, 1862, RG 156, misc. letters sent, E 3, vol 55, p. 200, Nat. Arch.; Stevens, p. 75; Ripley, p. 27; G.G. Benedict, op. cit., p. 755.

128. Stevens, p. 75; Ripley, p. 29; Aschmann, p. 63.

129. Mitchell, p. 263.

130. James G. Genco, *Arming Michigan's Regiments, 1862-1864,* pvt. publ., 1982, pp. 81-91 [from Summary Statements of Quarterly Returns, Ordnance and Ordnance Stores, RG 156, MI 1281, rolls 4-7, National Archives].

131. Stevens, pp. 119, 224, 369, 462.

132. Stevens, pp. 133, 163, 236; photographs of California Joe Head, Sept., 1862, Vermont Historical Society.

133. Stevens, pp. 203, 252, 311, 340, 360, 387, 417; Ripley, p. 158.

134. Stevens, pp. 310, 357; Ripley, p. 58.

135. Berdan to Frank S. Earle, A.A.A.G., Sept. 16, 1862, Hiram Berdan, personal service records, National Archives.

136. Sullivan Cook letter, Sept. 22, 1862, U. of Mich.; Stevens, p. 214.

137. Summary Statement of Quarterly Returns, Ordnance and Ordnance Stores, 1862-1867, RG 156, MI 1281, rolls 4-7, National Archives; Stevens, p. 205.

138. O.R. Howard Thompson, and William H. Rauch, *History of the Bucktails,* Philadelphia, 1906, pp. 142-143; Summary Statment Ordnance, MI 1281, rolls 4-7.

139. Caspar Trepp Papers, March 31, 1863 returns, 1st U.S.S.S., N.Y. Hist. Soc.

140. Caspar Trepp Papers, Return of Ordnance, 2d Quarter 1863, 3d Quarter, 1863, N.Y. Hist. Soc.

141. Caspar Trepp Papers, Statement on Ordnance Stores, Aug. 26, 1863, Armorer's Report, 1st U.S.S.S., Sept. 1863, N.Y. Hist. Soc.

142. Caspar Trepp Papers, March 31, 1863 return, Company G, 1st U.S.S.S., Certificate of Turn Ins, Oct. 10, 1863, N.Y. Hist. Soc.

143. McAulay, p. 84; Sellers, pp. 175-176; H. of Rep., Ex. Doc.,(U.S. 1338) pp. 945ff.

144. Stevens, p. 236.

145. see McAulay, pp. 73-74; Sellers, pp. 81-82.

146. G.T. Balch to Ripley, April 7, 1862, RG 156 E 21 #468; John Taylor to Ripley, April 23, 1862, RG 156, letters received, E 21, 1862, #393 T, National Archives; compiled reference notes, Sharps rifles, author's files.

147. Frank Sellers to author, Nov. 16, 1959; Sharps factory shipping ledgers, "Arms received and delivered by Sharps Rifle Manufacturing Company," 1863, Connecticut State Library, Hartford, Ct.

148. compiled reference notes, Sharps rifles and carbines, author's files.

BIBLIOGRAPHY

Manuscripts and Miscellaneous Documents:
Hiram Berdan, Court Martial Records, RG 153, LL188, March 3, 1863, National Archives, Washington, D.C.
Hiram Berdan, Military Service Records, National Archives, Washington, D.C.
Sullivan Cook, letters, Co. I. 1st U.S. Sharpshooters, 1862, University of Michigan, Bentley Historical Library, Ann Arbor.
Detroit Daily Advertiser, August 22, 1861
Detroit Free Press, Nov. 7, 1861; Nov. 8, 1861; Jan. 8, 1862; Jan. 24, 1862; Feb. 6, 1862.
Detroit Tribune, July 11, 1861; July 17, 1861; Nov. 23, 1861.
William B. Greene, diary, 1864, 1865, Co. G, 2d U.S. Sharpshooters, collection of Wiley Sword.
Inspection Reports, 1st U.S. Sharpshooters, Nov. 1, 1862; Dec. 19, 1862, RG 94, National Archives, Washington, D.C.
"Peirce's Sharp Shooters," recruiting brochure/poster, dated Columbus [Ohio], July 29, 1862, courtesy of Conrad Bush, Ft. Walton Beach, Florida.
Theodore Preston, letters, 1861 - 1862, Co. B, 2d U.S. Sharpshooters, University of Michigan, Bentley Historical Library, Ann Arbor.
Records of the Chief of Ordnance, RG 156; Records of the Secretary of War, RG 107; General Records (Adjutant General), National Archives, Washington, D.C.
Frank M. Sellers, letters to author, Nov. 16, 1959; March 5, 1960.
Sharps factory shipping ledgers, "Arms received and delivered by Sharps Rifle Manufacturing Company," 1863, Connecticut State Library, Hartford.
Sharps sales catalog, November 1, 1859 (reprint, 1960)
G.W. Smith, letter, Co. G, 1st U.S. Sharpshooters, Feb. 11, 1862, collection of Richard A. Johnson.
Caspar Trepp, Correspondence and Papers, 1861-1863, New York Historical Society, Albany.
Caspar Trepp, Court Martial Records, RG 153, LL 89, Feb. 19, 1863, National Archives, Washington, D.C.
Caspar Trepp, Military Service Records, National Archives, Washington, D.C.

Periodicals:
Richard F. Carlile, "The Sharps Rifle," *Military Images,* March/April, 1987, p. 6 ff.
Edward A. Hull, "Berdan Breechloaders," in seven parts, *The Gun Report,* March, 1986 - April 1987.
William C. Kent, "Sharpshooting with Berdan," *Civil War Times, Illustrated,* May, 1976, p. 4 ff.
Gary Kross, "'Rebel Yells' on Both Flanks," *Blue and Gray Magazine,* March, 1988, p. 4 ff.

Michael J. McAfee, "Sharpshooters, U.S. Army Uniforms of the Civil War, Part VII," *Military Images,* March/April, 1984, p. 5 ff.

C. Meade Patterson, "Martial Percussion Revolver Inspectors," Parts I, II, *The Gun Report,* March, 1960, April, 1960, p. 10 ff.

Richard A. Sauers, "Sickles - Right or Wrong," *Blue & Gray Magazine,* March, 1988, p. 56 ff.

Wiley Sword, "The Berdan Sharps Rifles," *Man at Arms,* May/June, 1979, p. 18 ff.

Wiley Sword, "The Berdan Sharps Rifle - An Update," *Man at Arms,* July/August, 1980, p. 38 ff.

Stuart G. Vogt, "'California Joe' Head," *Military Images,* March/April, 1984, p. 10 ff.

Books:

Rudolph Aschmann, *Three Years in the Army of the Potomac, or A Swiss Company of Sharpshooters in the North American War, in Memoirs of a Swiss Officer in the American Civil War,* Heinz K. Meier, ed., Bern, Switzerland, 1972.

G. G. Benedict, *Vermont in the Civil War, A History of the Part Taken By the Vermont Soldiers and Sailors in the War for the Union, 1861-5,* vol. II, Burlington, Vt., 1888, (reprint 1981).

Frederick H. Dyer, *A Compendium of the War of the Rebellion,* 3 vols., New York, 1959.

William F. Fox, *Regimental Losses in the American Civil War 1861 - 1865,* Albany, New York, 1898, (reprint: Dayton, Ohio, 1985).

James G. Genco, *Arming Michigan's Regiments, 1862 - 1864,* privately published, 1982.

House of Representatives, Executive Documents, US 1131 (#67 - 37:2); US 1338 (#99 v.12), Washington, D.C.

John Quinn Imholte, *The First Volunteers, History of the First Minnesota Volunteer Regiment 1861 - 1865,* Minneapolis, 1963.

John D. McAulay, *Civil War Breechloading Rifles,* Lincoln, R.I., 1987.

Roy Marcot, *Spencer Repeating Firearms,* Irvine, Calif., 1983

James L. Mitchell, *Colt, the Man, the Arms, the Company,* Harrisburg, Pa., 1959.

New York at Gettysburg, Final Report on the Battlefield of Gettysburg, vol. III, Albany, N.Y., 1900.

William Y.W. Ripley, *Vermont Riflemen in the War for the Union 1861 to 1865; A History of Company F, First United States Sharp-Shooters,* Rutland, Vt., 1883 (Grand Army Reprint, 1981).

Frank Sellers, *Sharps Firearms,* No. Hollywood, Calif., 1978.

Senate Executive Document, US 1123 (#72 - 37:2), Washington, D.C.

C.A. Stevens, *Berdan's United States Sharpshooters in the Army of the Potomac, 1861-1865,* St. Paul, Minn., 1882.

O.R. Howard Thompson, and William H. Rauch, *History of the Bucktails, Kane Rifle Regiment of the Pennsylvania Reserve Corps (13th Pennsylvania Reserves, 42nd of the Line),* Philadelphia, 1906.

War of the Rebellion: A Compiliation of the Official Records of the Union and Confederate Armies, 127 volumes and index, Washington, D.C., 1880 - 1901.

R. L. Wilson, *The Colt Heritage,* New York, 1979.

APPENDIX A:
DIARY (1864) OF PRIVATE WILLIAM B. GREEN, CO. G, 2D U.S. SHARPSHOOTERS

Any original diary from the Berdan Sharpshooters is genuinely rare, but due to the severe reduction in the number of men remaining in both regiments, during the final year of the war they are almost non-existent. William B. Greene was a veteran sharpshooter who had served from the very beginning of his regiment's active service, but had been wounded during the Second Bull Run Campaign. Because of mysterious circumstances which resulted in his being listed as a deserter, he did not return to active duty until more than a year later. Although he had missed the carnage at Antietam, Chancellorsville, and Gettysburg, Greene was present to witness a new and more devastating era of warfare, the modern phase of almost continuous fighting against an entrenched enemy — Grant's sledgehammer attacks and flanking maneuvers of 1864. Greene's portrayals of the arduous conditions and intense stress that seemed never to end are particularly suggestive of what it meant to be a sharpshooter at a time when so few were there to record their special ordeal. Greene's eye witness reports are all the more meaningful because he utilized supplementary journals to elaborate on the critical events as they occurred. Although an enlisted man, Private Greene was a good observer, and had a flair for reporting what was important.

William B. Greene, a student from Raymond, New Hampshire, was mustered into Company G, 2d U.S. Sharpshooters on December, 1861. Although listed as age 18, he had provided the written consent of his parents when he had originally enlisted on September 26th. He was described as only 5'7-1/2,' with blue eyes and brown hair. Following his wounding either at Brawner's Farm or Second Bull Run Greene was reported as in various hospitals. Yet on December 8, 1862 he was listed as a deserter from Lovell General Hospital, Portsmouth Grove, Rhode Island. There is no report of Greene thereafter until October 17, 1863, when he was arrested at Prairie du Chien, Wisconsin and sent under guard back to the 2d Sharpshooters in Virginia. Reported as present as of December 9, 1863, Greene was restored to duty by Maj. Gen. David Birney with only the term of nine months being added to his enlistment (the period he was AWOL). Apparently there were some extenuating circumstances involving his lengthy absence, for Private Greene was given a thirty day furlough for re-enlisting (along with a $400 bounty). It was during this furlough that Greene began his daily diary entries.

While periodic gaps occur due to sickness and routine duty, extensively covered are the periods of heavy fighting from the Wilderness through the Siege of Petersburg. Reported as sick from November 16, 1864, Greene apparently did not return to active duty although listed on the rolls of the 5th N.H. Battalion from February 15, 1865.

His two 1864 pocket size diaries show considerable surface wear from being carried in the field. The entries are nearly all in pencil, and Greene utilized a rather unique system under each daily entry. If more space were needed to elaborate, Greene continued the entry in the second diary which he referred to as "memoranda." Excerpts from the two 1864 diaries are as follows:

Fri. Feb.12, 1864

Been home since Jan. 11th on furlough which expired last night and I have reported at Concord [N.H.] where I am now stationed with the company.

Sun. March 27th, 1864

Left Concord for my Regt. in company with two of the 14th N.H.V. by way of Nashville & Wooster R.R. Took the boat at New London for N.Y.

Tues. March 29th

Arrived in Washington this morning & am stopping at soldier's retreat [.] Soldiers here being examined for commissions in nigger regts.

Thurs. March 31st

I visited the U.S. Capital to day & went in to the House of Representatives [and] into the Senate chamber, & c. I had a nice ice cream at the refreshment rooms[.] Went to Ford Theatre to night[.] Had a good play[.] Forrest is the chief actor[.]

Fri. April 22nd, 1864

Grand review of 2d & 3d Army Corps by Gen. Grant[,] Meade[,] & Hancock. Had a pleasant time of it[.]

Sat. April 23d

Target shooting by the brigade.

Wed. May 4th, 1864

Received marching orders last night & marched at 11 o'clock[.] Continued marching all night[.] Crossed the Rapidan this noon & camped at

Chancellorsville to night.
Thurs. May 5th
Left Chancellorsville this morn. & marched about five miles where we have entrenched our selves[.] The Vermont Brigade has been fighting this afternoon.
Fri. May 6th
Great battle of the campaign commenced yesterday afternoon[.] This morning the 1st div. 3d Corps was ordered to the front[.] The 2nd U.S.S.S. went up in a body & lost many men[.] Have fought all day[.] Charge[d] by Johnny's[.]
Sat. May 7th
Volunteered for a scout this morn & went three miles up the Fredricksburg plank[.] Had several close shots & lost one man in Co. D.
Sun, May 8th
Left my regt. last night in the confusion & have been a straggler all day[.]

Mon. May 9th
Came up with my regt. this noon & found them skirmishing on the front. This afternoon our batteries gave the enemy a good shelling[,] to which the Johnnys have replied killing two of [the] 1st R.I.B[attery]. Skirmished for their train.
Tues. May 10th
Heavy cannonading this morn[.] Marched about two miles & entrenched our selves & have had a hard fought battle resulting in victory for the Union arms.
Wed. May 11th
Have engaged the enemy's s.s. to day[.] No general engagement[.] Lt. Col. Stoughton wounded[.] Gen. Ward placed under arrest[.]
Thurs. May 12th
Marched all night last night in a round about way & succeeded in flanking the enemy in their works[.] Charged & captured them with little loss to us but heavy to the enemy[,] their dead being piled up in the entrenchments very thick — worse than any place on the Gettysburg battlefield[.] A capture of 5,700 prisoners was one of the events of the day[,] they throwing [away] their arms & jumping into our lines[.]
Fri. May 13th
No general engagement today[.] The day spent in burying the dead[,] caring for the wounded & c. Camped at Gen. Birney's H.Q.
Sat. May 14th

Been in reserve for the 1st U.S.S.S. & have had nothing in particular to do. The 1st S.S. have been in front engaging the enemy's s.s.

Sun. May 15th

I was detailed for s.s. duty this morning[,] went on post & after staying nearly two hours the 1 & 2 S.S. were recalled unbeknown to me & I came very near being taken prisoner. The enemy came up to the house in which I was stationed & I took leg bail for the rear & succeeded in making good my escape amid a shower of bullets[.] Was reported [as] a prisoner at my company & the boys were surprised to see me to night[.] Four men lost in the regt[,] one killed.

Wed. May 18th

Started last night & marched all night & until three o'clock to day when [we] went into camp near the C[ourt] H[ouse].

Thurs. May 19th

Been in camp all day[.] Sick in tent all day[.]

Fri. May 20th

Started last night & marched all night & part of the day toward Hanover Junction.

Sat. May 21st

Started last night & marched all night & all day to day[.] Met the enemy this noon & have followed them until night.

Sun. May 22d

Been on reserve picket all day at Carolina Poor Farm....

Mon May 23d

Started on a march this morn & have marched until noon[.] Met the enemy on the N. Annie [Anna] River... strongly entrenched[.] The 2d S.S. were deployed & done sharpshooting with them until about five o'clock[,] when Birney's div. went in & charged the line of works on the north side of the river & succeeded through a shower of shell[,] grape shot[,] & bullets in capturing them[.] Luthur Crane Co. G wounded through the body[,] the ball entering one side & coming out at the other [.] Capt. Barker, Co. D[,] was wounded — had a thigh broken with a piece of shell[.] I helped to carry him back & did not go to div. H.Q. to rejoin my regt. but laid down in an old house & was routed up about 2 p.m. by the patrol & had to go in the night[.] Slept in a hen coop.

Tues. May 24th

Has been an artillery fight mostly to day[.] The 20th Indiana charged across the river in a line of skirmishers & captured the enemy's breast works & fort. Upon gaining a foot hold across the river [our] troops were immediately pushed across the river & drove the enemy nearly two miles[.] The enemy had a cross fire on the bridge & every time [a] regt. passed they were shelled. The 2d S.S. laid quiet all day until after dark when we went to the front to strengthen the skirmish line[.] Stopped about an hour & soon returned[.] I camped in an old house & had a good nights rest[.]

Wed. May 25th

Co. G & C are detail[ed] to day to keep [a] rebel battery silenced[.] We went out as near as we could get (500 yards) & we kept at them all day[.] no fighting to day.

Thurs. May 26th

Been lying in entrenchments on the No. Annie all day[.] Supply train arrived to night & issued three days rations[.] The Union troops have been tearing up the Rail Road[,] burning the ties & bending the rails all day to day on the No. Annie River & I think Gen. Grant is to fall back to night [,] for every thing that will be of help to the enemy is being destroyed[.] The mortars arrived & got into position to day & gave the enemy a few shots[.]

Fri. May 27th

Started on a march last night about 9 o'clock[.] Recrossed the river & went about a mile & halted for a rest[.] I went to sleep & when I woke up I found it was broad daylight & that the regt. had not moved at all[.] We made coffee & at 10 o'clock we started again on a march[.]

Sat. May 28th

Marched until 12 o'clock last night & bivouack[ed.] Started again this morning about 7 & marched until 5 o'clock when we halted & threw up breastworks[.] At 3 o'clock we crossed the Pamunkey River which again brought the Army of the Potomac on the peninsula[.] We find plenty of hogs & forage &c.

Sun. May 29th

Have been lying behind entrenchments all day up to five o'clock when we started on a march. Marched three miles & went into park.

Mon. May 30th

We find the enemy in front this morning & we are building breastworks — or at least the 3d Me. Vols. are & the 1st S.S. are in front keeping their S.S. quiet. We are living in a ravine this forenoon but this afternoon our co. & Co. C went about a mile to the right & threw up cover for our selves & done sharpshooting until after dark when we returned to the ravine again.

Tues. May 31st

About 8 o'clock this morning Ward's Brigade headed by the 2nd U.S.S.S. in a line of skirmishers charged the first line of the enemy's works. The s.s. started down the hill amid a shower of bullets through the ravine & up another hill when they met the enemy[.] On they went over the breastworks[.] The enemy up & run in every direction. The regt. held the works 1/2 hour before the brigade came up to support us. The regt. captured fifty prisoners. Sergeant Fletcher of my company captured & took in five prisoners alone[.] Artillery was at once sent on & the s.s. advanced & dug pits where they have done sharp shooting all day & returned to the rear to stop to night[.] Alonso Blood of Co. G was wounded thru the mouth[.] Sarg't Norris Smith was wounded slightly in the knee[.] We had none killed in the regt. & few wounded.

Wed. June 1st, 1864

Returned to our old line of works this morning about 3 o'clock & have not been engaged to day[.]

Thur. June 2d

Started on a march last night about 11 & marched all night & until noon to day when we again found the enemy in force in our front[,] the 5th & 6th [Corps] engaging them[.] We went in to park & stopped until dark when we advanced about a mile & went into camp for the night[.]

Fri. June 3d

The artillery on both sides opened this morning & we were obliged to receive quite a mite [of] shelling about noon[.] We went on to the right flank & occupied works which our men had driven the enemy from & received orders that no more offensive operations were to be made against the enemy.

Sat. June 4th

Marched about two miles toward our left & camped.... Received another shelling to night[.] Drew rations for two days.

Sun. June 5th

Was detailed with the rest of my co. to go on [the] skirmish line this morning. As soon as we arrived at our picket post D.N. Smith advanced to gain a good position & run into the enemy picket line & received a bullet through the side — a very bad wound[.] About 3 o'clock an agreement was made between the two parties to have no more shooting that day[.] We then met [and] had quite a nice chat[.] Exchanged coffee for tobacco & c.[.] But about 7 o'clock the enemy broke the agreement & commenced firing along the whole line which was answered by us[.] The artillery on both sides commenced & it was quite warm for a while.

Mon. June 6th

Been lying in camp all day[.]

Tues. June 7th

Have been on skirmish line again all day & have not fired a gun. I have laid within 2 rods of a rebel rifle pit all day[.] Have not felt well — diarrhea.

Wed. June 8th

Been lying in camp all day. I went to the dr. & got some pills which caused a great deal of pain & I have been in misery all day[.] I feel as though I was going to have a fit of sickness but I hope not.

Thurs. June 9th

Been in camp all day[.] ... Co. D has been on detail to day[.] Corporal Sally killed — shot through the head.

Sat June 11th

Been in camp all day or nearly so[.] ... A bugler by the name of Warner was killed in camp by a rebel s.s.

Sun. June 12th

On picket all day & have not fired a shot[.] [I] am the right of the line[.] There have been considerable [firing]. W. H. Hackett was wounded through the side.

Mon. June 13th

Was relieved last night & went to camp & started on a march[.] Marched all night & all day to day. We crossed the Chickahominia [Chickahominy] River at Long's Ferry at 11-1/2 o'clock. Passed through Charles City about 3 o'clock P.M. & encamped one mile to the right of [the] James River at a place called Harrison's Bay at 7 o'clock.

Tues. June 14th

Marched to the river at 10 o'clock P.M. & parked[.] Waited about one hour & took the ferry boat & went three miles down the river[.] The boat fell into the channel & turned around & landed us nearly opposite the place we went on the boat[.] After crossing we marched about three miles & camped for the night. I found plenty of black cherries & had a good mite of them — the first of the season.

Wed. June 15th

Started on a march at 10 P.M. & marched all day & camped at 12 o'clock at night within 1-1/2 miles of Petersburg. ...We have had a very hard march.

Thurs. June 16th

Our regt. was ordered on to the skirmish line this morning early[,] after receiving quite a hard shelling where we had bivouacked for the night. ...Three regts. in our brigade charged these works & were repulsed with heavy loss. ... Our regt. was still kept in a line & was under all of the fire but lost but three men during the charge. ... During the charges this morning and night I never saw shell & shot fall & fly any thicker or faster & I hope I shall never again[.] We have lost 18 men & two officers wounded in the regt. to day[,] Capt Wright & Gurst[,] none killed.

Fri. June 17th

Cannonading was kept up nearly all night & at day light this morning the enemy tried to charge but were immediately repulsed & our boys charged on them & kept them retreating[.] [They] captured five pieces of artillery[,] horses & limbers & caissons[.] [We] drove them from their fort on the left & c.[.] During the charge as I was lying in what I called a secure position a piece of shell weighing 1/2 lb. struck me on the ankle joint & caused much pain & I find my self very lame to night[.] Our regt. was taken from the line on the left & sent to the right this moment, where they have been all day[.] About 5 o'clock P.M. Burnside ordered a charge of one of his divisions & made quite a mistake[. He] charged & ordered the left of our Corps to surrender [the right of way] & as it was in the day time it was corrected with out much loss.

Sat. June 18th

Been in the rear most all day on a/c of wound received by shell[.] Major Rowell was wounded to day through the leg — a flesh wound. Sargt H.A. Colby wounded. The first div. attempted to make a charge but got repulsed. The 1st Me H[eavy] A[rtillery]got cut up badly[.] Our wounded & dead lie between the two lines of breastworks & nothing can be done for them.

Sun. June 19th...

The regt has been on [the] skirmish line all day[.] Drew two days rations.

Mon. June 20th

Been at the rear all day[.] ...Our quartermaster, Lieut. Yoot[?][probably Benjamin F. Calef] had his horse shot by a stray bullet.

Tues. June 21st

Came to the rear last night & started on a flank movement by the left[.] Marched until 3 P.M. when our regt which was in advance of the 1st run in to a trap & received a volley from the enemy[.] They immediately jumped over the fence & pitched into them & drove them into their entrenchments[.] But on a/c of the right & left supports not coming [up we] were obliged to fall back & in so doing the colonel [Homer R. Stoughton] & Capt. [Samuel F.] Murray with about a dozen privates were captured[.] The col. had just arrived from the hospital this morning[.] David McCall[,] 1st Sargt. Co. C was among those captured.

Wed. June 22nd

The regt. rejoined the brigade last night & today we have been on the skirmish line watching a lot of reb cavalry[.] About 3 P.M. we unexpectedly found ourselves flanked[,] the enemy crying out to us to come in Yanks — we won't hurt you[.] But most of the boys struck to the rear[,] but some twenty were captured[.] A.J. Engel of Co. G was among them.

Thurs. June 23rd

Been on picket all day[.] One man wounded[.] There has been considerable firing on the line to day[.] We were relieved to night by the 1st Mass. H[eavy] A[rtillery].

Fri. June 24th

Camped in first line of breastworks with our brigade last night & this morning our brigade was relieved by the 1st brigade[,] 1st div. & we came to the rear where we have been all day.

Sun. June 26th

Laid in camp until noon when our regt. was ordered on the picket line to stop correspondence between our pickets & those of the enemy.

Mon. June 27th

Last night the brigade advanced to near the picket line & built a line of breastworks[.] Worked all night while our regt was sleeping.

Wed. June 29th

Moved camp this morning & laid out [our] company's street[.] Put up our tents in good shape & at four o'clock we were ordered to pack up every thing.

Thurs. June 30th

Been in camp all day[.] Drew one day's rations soft bread[.] Played bluff with Davis Jackson & Co. E fellow[,] $2.00 a head[.]

Fri. July 1st, 1864

Been on picket all day[.] Was relieved at 5 P.M. All quiet[,] no firing[.] Returned to camp.

Sat. July 2d

Been in camp all day[.] Washed my shirt for the first time since May 1st [.] The boys dug a well to day 15 feet deep & found splendid water.

Mon. July 4th

Been in camp all day[.] Has been quiet along the line to day[.] Quite a dull 4th of July.

Fri. July 8th

Been on detail to day to strengthen in front of breastworks[.] Worked all day[.] The enemy opened their guns & sent in fire shell among us to night.

Tues. July 12th

Left camp [at] 2 o'clock this morning[.] Was call[ed] up in the night to tear away breastworks[.] We marched 2 miles on the flank & have been here all day.

Wed. July 13th

Marched about two miles & stopped in rear of 9th Corps & have gone in to camp. ... Dug a well to night.

Thurs. July 14th

Been in camp all day[.] Was taken sick in the night last night & have not been well all day[.] Our Corps have gone to the front with nothing but haversacks & equipments[.] Left every thing in camp.

Tues. July 26th

Have been laying in camp since July 14 doing fatigue duty in the trenches. Received marching orders this morn & started at 4 o'clock P.M. toward City Point on the James River.

Wed July 27th

Marched all night last night[.] Crossed the Appomattox River on pontoons at 11 o'clock & the James at four. Met the enemy in force[.] The 110th P[a]. V[ols.] & 99th do [Pa. Vols.] deployed with our regt. as skirmishers & had quite a sharp engagement[.] The 110th['s] loss was large[.] The 1st div. captured one battery of four 20 lbs. Parrott guns[,] six caissons & the men of the battery. Our gun boats kept up a continual fire on them during the engagement[,] sending 120 & 200 lb shell[.] Came on picket on the left flank at 4 P.M., but the enemy are not very near[,] there being 2 divisions of Cavalry in our front.

Thurs, July 28th

Been on picket all day[.] Started toward the river just before dark.

Fri. August 5th, 1864

Stayed quietly in camp until almost dark when we were called out to resist a charge[.] The Johnnys charged & blew up one of our forts but got repulsed & so we came back again.

Sat. August 6th

On camp police to day[.] Policed all round the camp[.] Been copying memoranda to day[.]

Fri. August 12th

This afternoon at 2-1/2 o'clock we received orders to pack up & we had about five minutes to do so[.] Came to City Point where we arrived just at dark & went into camp[.] I started on ahead of the column & stopped at the 9th Corps hospital near the point to see the 11th N.H. band[.] ...I stopped about an hour[.] Got my supper.... It has been a very hot day[.] Men have dropped dead in the road in some instances[.] Warren Fletcher got arrested by the provost marshal for attempting to strike him with his gun[.]

Sat. August 13th

We marched to the river & went aboard the transport steamer Kent[.] Dropped down the river where we have laid all day waiting for the rest of the boys of the corps to embark[.] It is the opinion of many that we are all going to Washington[,] some to Atlanta & others that we are going to Mobile[,] but it is uncertain where we are going. We drew two days rations of pork[,] sugar & c.[.] Drew a few mackerel.

Sun. August 14th

All the boats started at ten o'clock last night & arrived this morning at Deep Bottom on the James[,] about 8 miles from City Point[,] where we left the boats about six o'clock[.] Went on shore & my regt. was at once deployed in a line of skirmishers & ordered to advance on a line of works in our front[,] supposed to be filled with the enemy[.] We advanced cautiously & when within one hundred yards we started on the double quick & arriving at the works expecting every moment to be fired into[.] But we found the works empty[.] We remained there until we had got breath & then advanced on to a road a few rods from the works[.] On this road we found the enemy pickets[,] who after firing a few shots fled....

Tues. August 16th

My company was detailed to go on picket last night but I being at the 3d N.H. V[ols.] when they went [out, I] did not go[.] I with King Cross endeavored to find them but did not & so camped in the woods.

Wed. August 17th

I returned to the regt. this morning & ... came to the picket line.... When we had got [al]most to the line we heard a large explosion & the air for a few minutes was filled with shell & pieces of boards[.] After we got to the line we found that a hole full of 64 lb. shells had accidentally caught fire & exploded[.] The shells were some captured from the Johnny with four 64 lb. — 8 inch sea coast howitzers which was used on our gun boats with considerable effect[.] No one was hurt although some of the boys was near by the explosion.

Thurs. August 18th

Been on picket all day[.] About five o'clock the enemy attacked our picket line at our right but got repulsed with loss[.] During the attack the enemy gave us a pretty good shelling but no one was hurt. The gun boats threw some of their large shell & silenced the enemy's batteries[,] which was strongly entrenched in a corn field....

Fri. August 19th

Last night we were relieved from picket about 12 o'clock[.] Came to the rear[,] crossed the James & Appomattox at Paint Rock & arrived in front of Petersburg where we relieved the 2d div. 9th Corps in the breastworks[.] ...It has rained all day hard & when I arrived here I was wet to the skin[.] I took up my quarters under one of the [tree] bow[s.] The enemy gave us a pretty good shelling to night[.] The picket line here is about 50 yards apart & as there is no shooting the enemy can be seen so as to see their features[.] Most of them are ragged & dirty.

Fri. August 26th...

To day the pickets of the contending armies have been exchanging papers, coffee for tobacco & c[.] I exchanged a lb. of coffee for a lb. of tobacco & a paper for the Richmond Whig[. I] sent it home to night.

Sat. August 27th

Came on picket last night[.] Had quite a shower in the night[.] Exchanging papers was commenced this morn.

Sun. September 4th, 1864

Nothing of importance has happened since Aug 27[th.] To day we received news of the capture of Atlanta Ga. by Sherman.

Mon. Sept. 5th

All the artillery on the Union line opened last night in salute for the capture of Atlanta[.]

Tues. November 15th, 1864

Came to division hospital this morning. Sent to the doctor. A pleasant day.

Fri. Nov. 18th

Entered 3d div., 2d Corps hospital City Point[,] Va. to night.

Sat. Nov. 26th

Entered Lincoln Hospital Washington D.C.

Fri. December 9th, 1864

Recommended by Dr. King this morning for a furlough for (30) thirty days.

Mon. Dec. 12th
Three years to day since I first entered U.S. service.

MEMORANDA
[page 2]
no. of gun 56438
[page 3]
no of rifle July 7th 56793
[page]
W.B. Greene in a/c with U.S. Government for clothings — Dec. 1863 1 pair pants/ 2 pair stockings/ 1 pair shoes/ 1 bean kilt woolen/2 pieces shelter/ turned in one piece shelter/ 1 knapsack[,] haversack (do)/ 1 canteen/ Jan. Feb. & March nothing/ April 1864/ 1 pair pants & shoes/ 1 knapsack/ 1 haversack & canteen/ 1 rubber blanket/ 2 forage caps/ June ['64] 1 pair stockings/ Aug. 1 pair stockings — amount received from government since date of enlistment is $55.81 up to Dec. 1863

APPENDIX B:
REPORT OF MAJOR GEORGE G. HASTINGS, 1ST U.S.S.S., OF THE BATTLE OF CHANCELLORSVILLE, MAY 3, 1863.

Major George H. Hastings was in command of a battalion of three companies of the 1st U.S.S.S., serving as skirmishers for the regiment on the morning of May 3d. His detailed account of the fighting in the III Corps sector is particularly graphic, and well illustrates the nature of the combat Berdan's Sharpshooters were typically involved in. Particularly noteworthy are Hastings' comments about the effect of superior fire-power, following from use of their Sharps breechloading rifles, even when opposed by much greater enemy numbers. This aspect was to revolutionize tactical dispositions when such lessons were finally grasped by various commanders. During the heavy fighting which he describes, Major Hastings was severely wounded in the hip after having two horses shot from under him. Due to his disabling wound Major Hastings was discharged October 31, 1863. His official report was submitted to Lieutenant Colonel Caspar Trepp, then commanding the 1st U.S. Sharpshooters, but apparently was never forwarded through government channels. It has remained unpublished among Trepp's papers following that officer's death at Mine Run, November 30, 1863. From the Caspar Trepp Papers, New York Historical Society.

Brooklyn [N.Y.]
May 26, 1862

Lieut. Col. C. Trepp
    Comdg Regt. U.S. Sharpshooters
Colonel:
...Early in the morning of that day [May 3, 1863] the regiment was posted in line of battle in the woods a few hundred yards west of the road leading from Chancellorsville to the U.S. Ford and south of the road which branches from the U.S. Ford road and leads to Ellis' Ford. The regiment fronted about west, or west by north. Two companies, B (Capt. [John] Wilson) and I (Capt. [James F] Covel) were by your orders deployed as skirmishers about one hundred and fifty yards in advance of the regiment and you put me in immediate command of these skirmishers. Before we became engaged with the enemy my line was reinforced by Co. C (Capt. [James H.] Baker). As my men were then deployed the distance between them was somewhat less than the usual five paces, perhaps not averaging more than three paces. The timber was small, but so close that it was impossible to see far in the woods, and though our artillery and infantry were engaged to the left and in front of my position, I could not see at what distance or with what effect. The supports in my rear were also out of sight [122d Pennsylvania Infantry]. It soon appeared to me that the musketry was getting gradually nearer, as if our troops were being pressed back and that the enemy were gaining ground on our right flank. From the sound of the musketry and the direction of some of the bullets which reached us I deduced it best to change front, and accordingly made "front about" northwest by battn. The enemy having driven back the troops in front of my line, advanced rapidly and confidently with a line of skirmishers firing, and a line of battle closely following — directly towards my front. We allowed them to approach very near so that the effect of our fire might be certain. The first volley

checked their advance, and we had not fired more than four or five rounds, when they broke and all fled precipitately. We pursued, firing deliberately, keeping our line even and unbroken, and captured many prisoners, whom I disarmed and sent to the rear, singly and in squads, in most cases without any guard, as I could not spare men for that purpose.

I sent an officer to obtain a support and he returned with the 122d Pa., which followed my skirmishers as we drove the enemy. The rebels being driven out of the woods, halted behind a line of entrenchments, from which they kept up a lively fire upon the woods, in the edge of which I halted my skirmishers. These entrenchments I judged to be our own [captured earlier], from their form as nearly as I could make it out through the smoke. As the enemy appeared to be in strong force behind these entrenchments and I knew of no troops in my support except the 122d Pa., which appeared to be very small in numbers, I did not consider it prudent to advance further without orders. From our position in the edge of the woods we were able to use our rifles effectively against such rebels as appeared above the parapet, and I felt confident that we could prevent their advance across the field. When my command had been in this position only a few minutes I received a wound which disabled me and compelled me to leave the field. I am unable to state at what hour this was, but it was yet quite early in the morning. The conduct of all of the officers and men under my command deserves the highest praise. They received the enemy's fire and advance[d] with the utmost coolness, holding their own fire until the rebels were close upon them, and then firing very rapidly, but evidently with careful aim and estimate of distance. The accuracy of their fire was evident from the large number of dead and wounded rebels we passed in our advance.

The complete and almost instant success of a mere line of skirmishers in turning back the enemy approaching in force, after they had been...up to that time steadily gaining ground against our troops, I confess, surprised me. How much of that success is to be attributed to the superior skill of these skirmishers as marksmen, how much to the rapidity with which their Sharps rifles can be loaded and fired, how much to the remarkable coolness and steadiness of the men themselves, and how much to the success of other troops at the same time cooperating with us on the right or elsewhere, I do not pretend to judge. The thickness of the woods prevented my seeing what relation my position bore to that of any considerable body of our other troops. You have already received reports from the several captains of the losses in killed and wounded in my com-

mand.
I have the honor to remain, colonel
very respectfully your obedient serv't
Geo. G. Hastings
Major, 1st U.S. Sharpshooters

Major Hastings provided a cover letter to Lieut. Col. Trepp in forwarding his report, which is included below. Of specific interest are his critical comments about Berdan and another unit, which is suggestive of how frequently such material was left out of official reports due to the prospect of political repercussions.

Brooklyn, 26 May '63
Dear Colonel:
I rec'd yesterday Nestor's letter of the 22d mentioning your wish to have me make a report of the part taken by my three companies in the action at Chancellorsville on the 3d. It is rather larger than I would like to have made out, but I could not condense all the facts known and do justice to the men. I suppose you wanted it only for your own information, but it being official you have a right to forward it. I did not state in the report that before the enemy advanced to within sight of us, some other troops of our division, I think part of Franklin's Brigade, including your old friends to the 122d [Pa. Inf.] who had been deployed in line in front of us, fell back, and Gen. Whipple found it impossible to make them make a stand where we were. They fell back behind us, out of my sight. The 122d was afterwards, as I have stated in the report, brought up as a support, but it appeared to be only a small part of it, and Gen. Whipple and Col. Franklin were at the front when I was hit. The general said to me: "I shall never forget the 3d Brigade." On my way to the rear after I was wounded, I met Berdan in the field but out of sight of the enemy. He arrived at the place on the road where I found our pack mules some time before his command got there. From the time I was sent forward to the skirmish line I did not see Hiram Berdan until I passed him at the rear, though I don't know that that proves anything against him, for during that time I saw no sharpshooters but my three companies. ....I authorized you to sign my name to any proper paper signed by yourself and others to the president recommending against Hiram Berdan's promotion or against his having the control of more sharpshooters.
Yours truly,
Geo. Hastings

INDEX

The writer would like to acknowledge the generous cooperation and assistance of many individuals, publications, and institutions who helped by providing much valuable information for this project. Those individuals deserving special mention include; Stuart G. Vogt, Richard F. Carlile, Roy Marcot, Herb Peck, Jr., Michael J. McAfee, Marie Melchiori, and Andrew Mowbray.

Any one with specific data or information to contribute on the Berdan Sharpshooters or their weapons is invited to write to the author in care of the publisher.